HISTORY & GEOGRAPHY 500
Teacher's Guide

Author:

Theresa Buskey, J.D.

Editor:

Alan Christopherson, M.S.

All maps in this book © Map Resources, unless otherwise stated.

Alpha Omega

PUBLICATIONS

804 N. 2nd Ave. E.
Rock Rapids, IA 51246-1759

HISTORY & GEOGRAPHY 500

LIFEPAC® Overview

HISTORY & GEOGRAPHY SCOPE & SEQUENCE

	Grade 1	Grade 2	Grade 3
UNIT 1	I AM A SPECIAL PERSON • God made me • You are God's child • All about you • Using proper manners	LOOKING BACK • Remembering last year • Learning about early times • The trail of the Native Americans • Symbols and historic places	U.S. GEOGRAPHY AND HISTORY STUDY SKILLS • Map skills • Resources • Community
UNIT 2	COMMUNICATING WITH SOUNDS • Sounds people make • Sounds that communicate • Communicating without sound • Communicating with God	SETTLING THE NEW WORLD • The first settlers • Colonies of the new world • War for Independence • Symbols and historic places	NEW ENGLAND STATES • ME, NH, VT, MA, RI, and CT • New England geography • New England resources • New England community
UNIT 3	I HAVE FEELINGS • I feel sad • I feel afraid • I feel happy • I have other feelings	A NEW GOVERNMENT FOR A NEW COUNTRY • A study of government • Creating a government • Our government • Symbols and historic places	MID-ATLANTIC STATES • NY, PA, NJ, DE, MD, and DC • Mid-Atlantic geography • Mid-Atlantic resources • Mid-Atlantic community
UNIT 4	I LIVE IN A FAMILY • My mother and father • My brothers and sisters • My grandparents • What my family does	GOVERNMENT UNDER THE CONSTITUTION • Article One—legislative branch • Article Two—executive branch • Article Three—judicial branch • Bill of Rights • Symbols and historic places	SOUTHERN ATLANTIC STATES • WV, VA, NC, SC, GA, and FL • Southern Atlantic geography • Southern Atlantic resources • Southern Atlantic community
UNIT 5	YOU AND GOD'S FAMILY • Getting ready in the morning • Walking to school • The school family • The church family	OUR GOVERNMENT CLOSE TO HOME • Our state governments • Our local governments • Citizens of the United States • Symbols and historic places	SOUTHERN STATES • KY, TN, MS, LA, AL, OK, TX, and AR • Southern geography • Southern resources • Southern community
UNIT 6	PLACES PEOPLE LIVE • Life on the farm • Life in the city • Life by the sea	WESTWARD—FROM THE ORIGINAL COLONIES • The United States grows • The Lewis and Clark Expedition • The Old Southwest • Symbols and historic places	GREAT LAKES STATES • OH, IN, IL, MI, WI, and MN • Great Lakes geography • Great Lakes resources • Great Lakes community
UNIT 7	COMMUNITY HELPERS • Firefighters and police officers • Doctors • City workers • Teachers and ministers	SETTLING THE FRONTIER • The Texas frontier • Westward expansion • Meet America's pioneers • Symbols and historic places	MIDWESTERN STATES • ND, SD, NE, KS, MO, and IA • Midwestern geography • Midwestern resources • Midwestern community
UNIT 8	I LOVE MY COUNTRY • America discovered • The Pilgrims • The United States begins • Respect for your country	EXPLORING AMERICA WITH MAPS • Directions on a map • Reading roads and symbols • Natural features • Symbols and historic places	MOUNTAIN STATES • MT, ID, WY, NV, UT, CO, AZ, and NM • Mountain geography • Mountain resources • Mountain community
UNIT 9	I LIVE IN THE WORLD • The globe • Countries • Friends in Mexico • Friends in Japan	PAST, PRESENT, AND FUTURE MAPS • City maps • Building maps • History of maps • Symbols and historic places	PACIFIC STATES • WA, OR, CA, AK, and HI • Pacific geography • Pacific resources • Pacific community
UNIT 10	THE WORLD AND YOU • You are special • Your family • Your school and church • Your world	REVIEW UNITED STATES HISTORY • The United States begins • Creating a government • Mapping the United States	U.S. GEOGRAPHY AND HISTORY REVIEW • U.S. geographical features • Eastern U.S. review • Western U.S. review

HISTORY & GEOGRAPHY SCOPE & SEQUENCE

Grade 4	Grade 5	Grade 6	
OUR EARTH • The surface of the earth • Early explorations of the earth • Exploring from space • Exploring the oceans	**A NEW WORLD** • Exploration of America • The first colonies • Conflict with Britain • Birth of the United States	**WORLD GEOGRAPHY** • Latitude and longitude • Western and eastern hemispheres • The southern hemisphere • Political and cultural regions	UNIT 1
SEAPORT CITIES • Sydney • Hong Kong • Istanbul • London	**A NEW NATION** • War for Independence • Life in America • A new form of government • The Nation's early years	**THE CRADLE OF CIVILIZATION** • Mesopotamia • The Land of Israel • The Nation of Israel • Egypt	UNIT 2
DESERT LANDS • What is a desert? • Where are the deserts? • How do people live in the desert?	**A TIME OF TESTING** • Louisiana Purchase • War of 1812 • Sectionalism • Improvements in trade & travel	**GREECE AND ROME** • Geography of the region • Beginning civilizations • Contributions to other civilizations • The influence of Christianity	UNIT 3
GRASSLANDS • Grasslands of the world • Ukraine • Kenya • Argentina	**A GROWING NATION** • Andrew Jackson's influence • Texas & Oregon • Mexican War • The Nation divides	**THE MIDDLE AGES** • The feudal system • Books and schools • The Crusades • Trade and architecture	UNIT 4
TROPICAL RAINFORESTS • Facts about rainforests • Rainforests of the world • The Amazon rainforest • The Congo rainforest	**A DIVIDED NATION** • Civil War • Reconstruction • Gilded Age • The need for reform	**SIX SOUTH AMERICAN COUNTRIES** • Brazil • Colombia • Venezuela • Three Guianas	UNIT 5
THE POLAR REGIONS • The polar regions: coldest places in the world • The Arctic polar region • The Antarctic polar region	**A CHANGING NATION** • Progressive reforms • Spanish-American War • World War I • Roaring Twenties	**OTHER AMERICAN COUNTRIES** • Ecuador and Peru • Bolivia and Uruguay • Paraguay and Argentina • Chile	UNIT 6
MOUNTAIN COUNTRIES • Peru—the Andes • The Incas and modern Peru • Nepal—the Himalayas • Switzerland—the Alps	**DEPRESSION AND WAR** • The Great Depression • War begins in Europe • War in Europe • War in the Pacific	**AFRICA** • Geography and cultures • Countries of northern Africa • Countries of central Africa • Countries of southern Africa	UNIT 7
ISLAND COUNTRIES • Islands of the earth • Cuba • Iceland • Japan	**COLD WAR** • Korean War & other crises • Vietnam War • Civil Rights movement • Upheaval in America	**MODERN WESTERN EUROPE** • The Renaissance • The Industrial Revolution • World War I • World War II	UNIT 8
NORTH AMERICA • Geography • Lands, lakes, and rivers • Northern countries • Southern countries	**THE END OF THE MILLENNIUM** • Watergate and Détente • The fall of communism • Persian Gulf War • Issues of the new millennium	**MODERN EASTERN EUROPE** • Early government • Early churches • Early countries • Modern countries	UNIT 9
OUR WORLD IN REVIEW • Europe and the explorers • Asia and Africa • Southern continents • North America, North Pole	**THE UNITED STATES OF AMERICA** • Beginning America until 1830 • Stronger America 1830-1930 • 1930 to the end of the millennium • The new millennium	**THE DEVELOPMENT OF OUR WORLD** • Cradle of civilization • The Middle Ages • Modern Europe • South America and Africa	UNIT 10

HISTORY & GEOGRAPHY SCOPE & SEQUENCE

	Grade 7	Grade 8	Grade 9
UNIT 1	WHAT IS HISTORY • Definition and significance of history • Historians and the historical method • Views of history	EUROPE COMES TO AMERICA • Voyages of Columbus • Spanish exploration • Other exploration • The first colonies	UNITED STATES HERITAGE • American colonies • Acquisitions and annexations • Backgrounds to freedom • Backgrounds to society
UNIT 2	WHAT IS GEOGRAPHY • Classes of geography • Geography and relief of the earth • Maps and the study of our world • Time zones	BRITISH AMERICA • English colonies • Government • Lifestyle • Wars with France	OUR NATIONAL GOVERNMENT • Ideals of national government • National government developed • Legislative and executive branches • Judicial branch
UNIT 3	U.S. HISTORY AND GEOGRAPHY • Geography of the U.S. • Early history of the U.S. • Physical regions of the U.S. • Cultural regions of the U.S.	THE AMERICAN REVOLUTION • British control • Rebellion of the Colonies • War for independence • Constitution	STATE AND LOCAL GOVERNMENT • Powers of state government • County government • Township government • City government
UNIT 4	ANTHROPOLOGY • Understanding anthropology • The unity of man • The diversity of man • The culture of man	A FIRM FOUNDATION • Washington's presidency • Adams administration • Jeffersonian Democracy • War of 1812	PLANNING A CAREER • Definition of a career • God's will concerning a career • Selecting a career • Preparation for a career
UNIT 5	SOCIOLOGY • Sociology defined • Historical development • Importance to Christians • Method of sociology	A GROWING NATION • Jacksonian Era • Northern border • Southern border • Industrial Revolution	CITIZENSHIP • Citizenship defined • Gaining citizenship • Rights of citizenship • Responsibilities of citizenship
UNIT 6	U.S. ANTHROPOLOGY • Cultural background of the U.S. • Native American cultures • Cultures from distant lands • Cultural and social interaction	THE CIVIL WAR • Division & Secession • Civil War • Death of Lincoln • Reconstruction	THE EARTH AND MAN • Man inhabits the earth • Man's home on the earth • Man develops the earth • The future of the earth
UNIT 7	ECONOMICS • Economics defined • Methods of the economist • Tools of the economist • An experiment in economy	GILDED AGE TO PROGRESSIVE ERA • Rise of industry • Wild West • America as a world power • Progressive era	REGIONS OF THE WORLD • A region defined • Geographic and climate regions • Cultural and political regions • Economic regions of Europe
UNIT 8	POLITICAL SCIENCE • Definition of political science • Roots of Western thought • Modern political thinkers • Political theory	A WORLD IN CONFLICT • World War I • Great Depression • New Deal • World War II	MAN AND HIS ENVIRONMENT • The physical environment • Drug abuse • The social environment • Man's responsibilities
UNIT 9	STATE ECONOMICS AND POLITICS • Background of state government • State government • State finance • State politics	COLD WAR AMERICA • Origins of the Cold War • Vietnam • Truman to Nixon • Ending of the Cold War	TOOLS OF THE GEOGRAPHER • The globe • Types of maps • Reading maps • The earth in symbol form
UNIT 10	SOCIAL SCIENCES REVIEW • History and geography • Anthropology • Sociology • Economics and politics	RECENT AMERICA & REVIEW • Europe to independence • Colonies to the Civil War • Civil War to World War II • World War II through Cold War	MAN IN A CHANGING WORLD • Development of the nation • Development of government • Development of the earth • Solving problems

HISTORY & GEOGRAPHY SCOPE & SEQUENCE

Grade 10	Grade 11	Grade 12	
ANCIENT CIVILIZATION • Origin of civilization • Early Egypt • Assyria and Babylonia • Persian civilization	FOUNDATIONS OF DEMOCRACY • Democracy develops • Virginia • New England colonies • Middle and southern colonies	INTRODUCTION TO GOVERNMENTS • Why have governments • Types of governments • Governments in our world • Political thinkers	UNIT 1
ANCIENT CIVILIZATIONS • India • China • Greek civilization • Roman Empire	CONSTITUTIONAL GOVERNMENT • Relations with England • The Revolutionary War • Articles of Confederation • Constitution of the U.S.	UNITED STATES GOVERNMENT • U.S. Constitution • Bill of Rights • Three branches of government • Legislative process	UNIT 2
THE MEDIEVAL WORLD • Early Middle Ages • Middle Ages in transition • High Middle Ages	NATIONAL EXPANSION • A strong federal government • Revolution of 1800 • War of 1812 • Nationalism and sectionalism	AMERICAN PARTY SYSTEM • American party system • Development political parties • Functions of political parties • Voting	UNIT 3
RENAISSANCE AND REFORMATION • Changes in government and art • Changes in literature and thought • Advances in science • Reform within the Church	A NATION DIVIDED • Issues of division • Division of land and people • Economics of slavery • Politics of slavery	HISTORY OF GOVERNMENTS • Primitive governments • Beginnings of Democracy • Feudalism, Theocracy, & Democracy • Fascism & Nazism	UNIT 4
GROWTH OF WORLD EMPIRES • England and France • Portugal and Spain • Austria and Germany • Italy and the Ottoman Empire	A NATION UNITED AGAIN • Regionalism • The division • The Civil War • Reconstruction	THE CHRISTIAN AND HIS GOVERNMENT • Discrimination & the Christian • Christian attitudes • "Opinion & Truth" in politics • Politics & Propaganda	UNIT 5
THE AGE OF REVOLUTION • Factors leading to revolution • The English Revolution • The American Revolution • The French Revolution	INVOLVEMENT AT HOME & ABROAD • Surge of industry • The industrial lifestyle • Isolationism • Involvement in conflict	FREE ENTERPRISE • Economics • Competition • Money through history • International finance & currency	UNIT 6
THE INDUSTRIAL REVOLUTION • Sparks of preparation • Industrial revolution in England • Industrial revolution in America • Social changes of the revolution	THE SEARCH FOR PEACE • The War and its aftermath • The Golden Twenties • The Great Depression • The New Deal	BUSINESS AND YOU • Running a business • Government & business • Banks & Mergers • Deregulation & Bankruptcy	UNIT 7
TWO WORLD WARS • Mounting tension • World War I • Peace and power quests • World War II	A NATION AT WAR • Causes of the war • World War II • Korean Conflict • Vietnam Conflict	THE STOCK MARKET • How it started and works • Selecting stocks • Types of stocks • Tracking stocks	UNIT 8
THE CONTEMPORARY WORLD • The Cold War • Korean War and Vietnam War • Collapse of the Soviet Union • Today's world	CONTEMPORARY AMERICA • America in the 1960s • America in the 1970s • America in the 1980s & 90s • International Scene 1980-Present	BUDGET AND FINANCE • Cash, Credit & Checking • Buying a car • Grants, Loans, & IRAs • Savings & E-cash	UNIT 9
ANCIENT TIMES TO THE PRESENT • Ancient civilizations • Medieval times • The Renaissance • The modern world	UNITED STATES HISTORY • Basis of democracy • The 1800s • Industrialization • Current history	GEOGRAPHY • Euro & International finance • U.S. Geography • The global traveler • Neighbors, Heroes, & the Holy Land	UNIT 10

STRUCTURE OF THE LIFEPAC CURRICULUM

The LIFEPAC curriculum is conveniently structured to provide one Teacher's Guide containing teacher support material with answer keys and ten student worktexts for each subject at grade levels 2 through 12. The worktext format of the LIFEPACs allows the student to read the textual information and complete workbook activities all in the same booklet. The easy-to-follow LIFEPAC numbering system lists the grade as the first number(s) and the last two digits as the number of the series. For example, the Language Arts LIFEPAC at the 6th grade level, 5th book in the series would be LAN0605.

Each LIFEPAC is divided into three to five sections and begins with an introduction or overview of the booklet as well as a series of specific learning objectives to give a purpose to the study of the LIFEPAC. The introduction and objectives are followed by a vocabulary section which may be found at the beginning of each section at the lower levels or in the glossary at the high school level. Vocabulary words are used to develop word recognition and should not be confused with the spelling words introduced later in the LIFEPAC. The student should learn all vocabulary words before working the LIFEPAC sections to improve comprehension, retention, and reading skills.

Each activity or written assignment in grades 2 through 12 has a number for easy identification, such as 1.1. The first number corresponds to the LIFEPAC section and the number to the right of the decimal is the number of the activity.

Teacher checkpoints, which are essential to maintain quality learning, are found at various locations throughout the LIFEPAC. The teacher should check 1) neatness of work and penmanship, 2) quality of understanding (tested with a short oral quiz), 3) thoroughness of answers (complete sentences and paragraphs, correct spelling, etc.), 4) completion of activities (no blank spaces), and 5) accuracy of answers as compared to the answer key (all answers correct).

The self test questions in grades 2 through 12 are also number coded for easy reference. For example, 2.015 means that this is the 15th question in the self test of Section 2. The first number corresponds to the LIFEPAC section, the zero indicates that it is a self test question, and the number to the right of the zero the question number.

The LIFEPAC test is packaged at the center of each LIFEPAC. It should be removed and put aside before giving the booklet to the student for study.

Answer and test keys in grades 2 through 12 have the same numbering system as the LIFEPACs. The student may be given access to the answer keys (not the test keys) under teacher supervision so that he can score his own work.

A thorough study of the Scope & Sequence by the teacher before instruction begins is essential to the success of the student. The teacher should become familiar with expected skill mastery and understand how these grade-level skills fit into the overall skill development of the curriculum. The teacher should also preview the objectives that appear at the beginning of each LIFEPAC for additional preparation and planning.

TEST SCORING AND GRADING

Answer keys and test keys give examples of correct answers. They convey the idea, but the student may use many ways to express a correct answer. The teacher should check for the essence of the answer, not for the exact wording. Many questions are high level and require thinking and creativity on the part of the student. Each answer should be scored based on whether or not the main idea written by the student matches the model example. "Any Order" or "Either Order" in a key indicates that no particular order is necessary to be correct.

Most self tests and LIFEPAC tests at the lower elementary levels are scored at 1 point per answer; however, the upper levels may have a point system awarding 2 to 5 points for various answers or questions. Further, the total test points will vary; they may not always equal 100 points. They may be 78, 85, 100, 105, etc.

Example 1

Example 2

A score box similar to ex. 1 above is located at the end of each self test and on the front of the LIFEPAC test. The bottom score, 72, represents the total number of points possible on the test. The upper score, 58, represents the number of points your student will need to receive an 80% or passing grade. If you wish to establish the exact percentage that your student has achieved, find the total points of his correct answers and divide it by the bottom number (in this case 72). For example, if your student has a point total of 65, divide 65 by 72 for a grade of 90%. Referring to ex. 2, on a test with a total of 105 possible points, the student would have to receive a minimum of 84 correct points for an 80% or passing grade. If your student has received 93 points, simply divide the 93 by 105 for a percentage grade of 89%. Students who receive a score below 80% should review the LIFEPAC and retest using the appropriate Alternate Test found in the Teacher's Guide.

The following is a guideline to assign letter grades for completed LIFEPACs based on a maximum total score of 100 points.

Example:

LIFEPAC Test	=	60% of the Total Score (or percent grade)
Self Test	=	25% of the Total Score (average percent of self tests)
Reports	=	10% or 10* points per LIFEPAC
Oral Work	=	5% or 5* points per LIFEPAC

*Determined by the teacher's subjective evaluation of the student's daily work.

Example:

LIFEPAC Test Score	=	92%	92 × .60	=	55 points
Self Test Average	=	90%	90 × .25	=	23 points
Reports				=	8 points
Oral Work				=	4 points
TOTAL POINTS				=	90 points

Grade Scale based on point system:

100 – 94	=	A
93 – 86	=	B
85 – 77	=	C
76 – 70	=	D
Below 70	=	F

TEACHER HINTS AND STUDYING TECHNIQUES

LIFEPAC activities are written to check the level of understanding of the preceding text. The student may look back to the text as necessary to complete these activities; however, a student should never attempt to do the activities without reading (studying) the text first. Self tests and LIFEPAC tests are never open book tests.

Language arts activities (skill integration) often appear within other subject curriculum. The purpose is to give the student an opportunity to test his skill mastery outside of the context in which it was presented.

Writing complete answers (paragraphs) to some questions is an integral part of the LIFEPAC curriculum in all subjects. This builds communication and organization skills, increases understanding and retention of ideas, and helps enforce good penmanship. Complete sentences should be encouraged for this type of activity. Obviously, single words or phrases do not meet the intent of the activity, since multiple lines are given for the response.

Review is essential to student success. Time invested in review where review is suggested will be time saved in correcting errors later. Self tests, unlike the section activities, are closed book. This procedure helps to identify weaknesses before they become too great to overcome. Certain objectives from self tests are cumulative and test previous sections; therefore, good preparation for a self test must include all material studied up to that testing point.

The following procedure checklist has been found to be successful in developing good study habits in the LIFEPAC curriculum.

1. Read the introduction and Table of Contents.
2. Read the objectives.
3. Recite and study the entire vocabulary (glossary) list.
4. Study each section as follows:
   a. Read the introduction and study the section objectives.
   b. Read all the text for the entire section, but answer none of the activities.
   c. Return to the beginning of the section and memorize each vocabulary word and definition.
   d. Reread the section, complete the activities, check the answers with the answer key, correct all errors, and have the teacher check.
   e. Read the self test but do not answer the questions.
   f. Go to the beginning of the first section and reread the text and answers to the activities up to the self test you have not yet done.
   g. Answer the questions to the self test without looking back.
   h. Have the self test checked by the teacher.
   i. Correct the self test and have the teacher check the corrections.
   j. Repeat steps a–i for each section.
5. Use the **SQ3R** method to prepare for the LIFEPAC test.
   > **S**can the whole LIFEPAC.
   > **Q**uestion yourself on the objectives.
   > **R**ead the whole LIFEPAC again.
   > **R**ecite through an oral examination.
   > **R**eview weak areas.
6. Take the LIFEPAC test as a closed book test.
7. LIFEPAC tests are administered and scored under direct teacher supervision. Students who receive scores below 80% should review the LIFEPAC using the **SQ3R** study method and take the Alternate Test located in the Teacher's Guide. The final test grade may be the grade on the Alternate Test or an average of the grades from the original LIFEPAC test and the Alternate Test.

GOAL SETTING AND SCHEDULES

Each school must develop its own schedule, because no single set of procedures will fit every situation. The following is an example of a daily schedule that includes the five LIFEPAC subjects as well as time slotted for special activities.

Possible Daily Schedule

8:15	–	8:25	Pledges, prayer, songs, devotions, etc.
8:25	–	9:10	Bible
9:10	–	9:55	Language Arts
9:55	–	10:15	Recess (juice break)
10:15	–	11:00	Math
11:00	–	11:45	History & Geography
11:45	–	12:30	Lunch, recess, quiet time
12:30	–	1:15	Science
1:15	–		Drill, remedial work, enrichment*

*Enrichment: *Computer time, physical education, field trips, fun reading, games and puzzles, family business, hobbies, resource persons, guests, crafts, creative work, electives, music appreciation, projects.*

Basically, two factors need to be considered when assigning work to a student in the LIFEPAC curriculum.

The first is time. An average of 45 minutes should be devoted to each subject, each day. Remember, this is only an average. Because of extenuating circumstances a student may spend only 15 minutes on a subject one day and the next day spend 90 minutes on the same subject.

The second factor is the number of pages to be worked in each subject. A single LIFEPAC is designed to take three to four weeks to complete. Allowing about three to four days for LIFEPAC introduction, review, and tests, the student has approximately 15 days to complete the LIFEPAC pages. Simply take the number of pages in the LIFEPAC, divide it by 15 and you will have the number of pages that must be completed on a daily basis to keep the student on schedule. For example, a LIFEPAC containing 45 pages will require three completed pages per day. Again, this is only an average. While working a 45-page LIFEPAC, the student may complete only one page the first day if the text has a lot of activities or reports, but go on to complete five pages the next day.

Long-range planning requires some organization. Because the traditional school year originates in the early fall of one year and continues to late spring of the following year, a calendar should be devised that covers this period of time. Approximate beginning and completion dates can be noted on the calendar as well as special occasions such as holidays, vacations and birthdays. Since each LIFEPAC takes three to four weeks or 18 days to complete, it should take about 180 school days to finish a set of ten LIFEPACs. Starting at the beginning school date, mark off 18 school days on the calendar and that will become the targeted completion date for the first LIFEPAC. Continue marking the calendar until you have established dates for the remaining nine LIFEPACs making adjustments for previously noted holidays and vacations. If all five subjects are being used, the ten established target dates should be the same for the LIFEPACs in each subject.

TEACHING SUPPLEMENTS

The sample weekly lesson plan and student grading sheet forms are included in this section as teacher support materials and may be duplicated at the convenience of the teacher.

The student grading sheet is provided for those who desire to follow the suggested guidelines for assignment of letter grades as previously discussed. The student's self test scores should be posted as percentage grades. When the LIFEPAC is completed the teacher should average the self test grades, multiply the average by .25 and post the points in the box marked self test points. The LIFEPAC percentage grade should be multiplied by .60 and posted. Next, the teacher should award and post points for written reports and oral work. A report may be any type of written work assigned to the student whether it is a LIFEPAC or additional learning activity. Oral work includes the student's ability to respond orally to questions which may or may not be related to LIFEPAC activities or any type of oral report assigned by the teacher. The points may then be totaled and a final grade entered along with the date that the LIFEPAC was completed.

The Student Record Book, which was specifically designed for use with the Alpha Omega curriculum, provides space to record weekly progress for one student over a nine-week period as well as a place to post self test and LIFEPAC scores. The Student Record Books are available through the current Alpha Omega catalog; however, unlike the enclosed forms, these books are not for duplication and should be purchased in sets of four to cover a full academic year.

WEEKLY LESSON PLANNER

Week of:

	Subject	Subject	Subject	Subject
Monday				
Tuesday	Subject	Subject	Subject	Subject
Wednesday	Subject	Subject	Subject	Subject
Thursday	Subject	Subject	Subject	Subject
Friday	Subject	Subject	Subject	Subject

WEEKLY LESSON PLANNER

Week of:

	Subject	Subject	Subject	Subject
Monday				
	Subject	Subject	Subject	Subject
Tuesday				
	Subject	Subject	Subject	Subject
Wednesday				
	Subject	Subject	Subject	Subject
Thursday				
	Subject	Subject	Subject	Subject
Friday				

Student Name _____   Year _____

Bible

LP	Self Test Scores by Sections 1	2	3	4	5	Self Test Points	LIFEPAC Test	Oral Points	Report Points	Final Grade	Date
01											
02											
03											
04											
05											
06											
07											
08											
09											
10											

History & Geography

LP	Self Test Scores by Sections 1	2	3	4	5	Self Test Points	LIFEPAC Test	Oral Points	Report Points	Final Grade	Date
01											
02											
03											
04											
05											
06											
07											
08											
09											
10											

Language Arts

LP	Self Test Scores by Sections 1	2	3	4	5	Self Test Points	LIFEPAC Test	Oral Points	Report Points	Final Grade	Date
01											
02											
03											
04											
05											
06											
07											
08											
09											
10											

Student Name _____   Year _____

Math

LP	Self Test Scores by Sections 1	2	3	4	5	Self Test Points	LIFEPAC Test	Oral Points	Report Points	Final Grade	Date
01											
02											
03											
04											
05											
06											
07											
08											
09											
10											

Science

LP	Self Test Scores by Sections 1	2	3	4	5	Self Test Points	LIFEPAC Test	Oral Points	Report Points	Final Grade	Date
01											
02											
03											
04											
05											
06											
07											
08											
09											
10											

Spelling/Electives

LP	Self Test Scores by Sections 1	2	3	4	5	Self Test Points	LIFEPAC Test	Oral Points	Report Points	Final Grade	Date
01											
02											
03											
04											
05											
06											
07											
08											
09											
10											

INSTRUCTIONS FOR HISTORY & GEOGRAPHY

The LIFEPAC curriculum from grades 2 through 12 is structured so that the daily instructional material is written directly into the LIFEPACs. The student is encouraged to read and follow this instructional material in order to develop independent study habits. The teacher should introduce the LIFEPAC to the student, set a required completion schedule, complete teacher checks, be available for questions regarding both content and procedures, administer and grade tests, and develop additional learning activities as desired. Teachers working with several students may schedule their time so that students are assigned to a quiet work activity when it is necessary to spend instructional time with one particular student.

The Teacher Notes section of the Teacher's Guide lists the required or suggested materials for the LIFEPACs and provides additional learning activities for the students. The materials section refers only to LIFEPAC materials and does not include materials which may be needed for the additional activities. Additional learning activities provide a change from the daily school routine, encourage the student's interest in learning, and may be used as a reward for good study habits.

ADDITIONAL PROJECTS OR INFORMATION FOR ALL LIFEPACS

» IN GENERAL

1. Check to see if there are any "living history" exhibits in your area (Rebuilt towns from history in which people demonstrate how Americans lived at that time). Plan a field trip to the site when the students are studying that time period.

2. Do the history of your state as a second course or, with fewer requirements, as course enrichment. Start a notebook for your state. Start with its symbols and flag. For each section you study in the LIFEPAC, research what was happening in your state at that time. Put notes on those things in the book. Include Native American tribes, European or American settlement, statehood, war battles, reforms, leaders, etc.

» ON THE INTERNET

The Additional Learning Activities found under the Teacher Notes for each LIFEPAC include "Explore the Internet" activities. For most of these activities, key terms or phrases are included to help the student(s) search for websites on various historical topics. On occasion, a particular website will be suggested. Be sure to monitor the websites the student(s) choose to visit.

HISTORY & GEOGRAPHY 501

Unit 1: A New World

TEACHER NOTES

MATERIALS NEEDED FOR LIFEPAC	
Required	Suggested
(None)	• globe or world map

ADDITIONAL LEARNING ACTIVITIES

Section 1: European Explorers

1. Do a class project on the Vikings: put up pictures you find; read about their lives; mark where they traveled on a map; mark off how big a long boat would be and put the class into it or plan an imaginary Viking voyage of exploration from Iceland or Greenland with Eric the Red or Leif Ericson.

2. Teacher: Many modern historians have stopped using B.C. and A.D. for dates. They use B.C.E. (Before Common Era) and C.E. (Common Era) to avoid any reference to Jesus. Discuss with your class why they would do this.

3. Do a report or project on a Native-American tribe near you.

4. Discuss spices in class. Have the students find out which ones their parents use. Then, find out where those spices come from.

5. On your world map trace some of the trade routes from Europe to Asia. Discuss the problems traders might find on each route.

6. Do a one- to two-page paper or an oral report on the life of an explorer.

Section 2: English Colonies

1. Read a fiction book about someone in the American colonies.

2. Explore the Internet to discover more about colonial settlements. Visit the websites of these two living history museums: Colonial Williamsburg and Plymoth Plantation (notice the special spelling of this site).

3. Do a one- to two-page paper or an oral report on an early American colonist. (Suggestions: John Winthrop, John Smith, Roger Williams, Thomas Hooker or William Penn).

4. Choose a colony. Look up more information on the religious life in that colony. Discuss it with the class.

5. Build a model of a colonial town or plantation.

6. Discuss these questions with the class:

   a. Why would people choose to come to America?

   b. What part of the colonies would you like to have lived in?

    c. What would it be like to come to America as an indentured servant?

    d. How would you have set up a colony if you were given a charter?

7. Look up information on Puritans, Separatists, Quakers and Catholics. Learn why and how they were persecuted in England.

Section 3: Revolution Begins

1. Look up information on the Great Awakening. Share with the class what you learn.

2. Do a one- to two-page paper or an oral report on a battle in the French and Indian War.

3. Discuss these questions in class:

    a. Why was the French and Indian War so important in American history?

    b. How were the colonial governments similar to the government in the United States today?

    c. Why didn't the Americans and British negotiate over their problems?

    d. What would you have thought about the American tax revolt if you were an official in the British government?

    e. Why were the Americans so upset about the Stamp Act?

    f. Was it right or wrong for the Americans to revolt?

4. Read about George Washington's life during the French and Indian War. Discuss with the class what he learned that would help him as commander-in-chief of the American army and president of the United States.

5. Draw a diagram or make a model of the battle of Lexington, Concord or Bunker Hill.

6. Class project: Find a list of the men who attended the First or Second Continental Congress. Assign a student to read about one man and what he went on to do in the new United States. Have the students present their information to the class.

7. Do a paper or oral report on the weapons used in wars in the late 1700s.

8. Read "Paul Revere's Ride" by Henry Wadsworth Longfellow aloud.

9. Pretend you are living in Boston in 1765 and plan a protest against the Stamp Act. Make signs to carry and slogans to shout.

10. Read the Declaration of Independence aloud in class and discuss it.

Administer the LIFEPAC Test.

The test is to be administered in one session. Give no help except with directions.
Evaluate the tests and review areas where the students have done poorly.
Review the pages and activities that stress the concepts tested.
If necessary, administer the Alternate LIFEPAC Test.

ANSWER KEYS

SECTION 1

1.1	f, p
1.2	b
1.3	o
1.4	d, m
1.5	e, j
1.6	c, q, r
1.7	a
1.8	g, k
1.9	h
1.10	n
1.11	i, l
1.12	Spain
1.13	San Salvador; 1492
1.14	Asia; America
1.15	West Indies
1.16	Isabela; Hispaniola
1.17	Asia
1.18	Any order: *Niña, Pinta, Santa Maria*
1.19	four
1.20	b
1.21	c
1.22	a
1.23	e
1.24	d
1.25	f
1.26	Northwest
1.27	Mississippi
1.28	Algonquin; Iroquois
1.29	Quebec
1.30	Champlain
1.31	Louisiana
1.32	fur

1.33 & 1.34

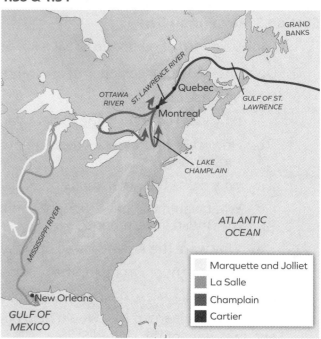

1.35	Francis Drake
1.36	New Amsterdam
1.37	Henry Hudson
1.38	Roanoke
1.39	John Cabot
1.40	New York
1.41	Manhattan
1.42	Dutch West India Co.

SELF TEST 1

1.01   ACROSS   DOWN
     2. Champlain   1. Magellan
     4. Hudson   2. Coronado
     6. Joliet   3. Cartier
     7. Leon   5. Columbus
     8. Drake
     9. Cabot
     10. DeSoto

1.02   Leif Ericson
1.03   spices
1.04   Henry
1.05   1492; Any order: *Pinta, Santa Maria*
1.06   St. Augustine; Spain
1.07   Northwest
1.08   fur
1.09   Roanoke
1.010 West India
1.011 New York
1.012 Asia
1.013 Portugal
1.014 true
1.015 false
1.016 true
1.017 false
1.018 true
1.019 true
1.020 true

SECTION 2

2.1   John Rolfe
2.2   charter
2.3   1607
2.4   Pocahontas
2.5   indentured servant
2.6   head right system
2.7   starving time
2.8   tobacco
2.9   Virginia Co. of London
2.10 House of Burgesses
2.11 Any order: women, slaves
2.12 Pilgrims
2.13 *Mayflower*
2.14 The Mayflower Compact
2.15 Squanto
2.16 no
2.17 the first Thanksgiving
2.18 Virginia
2.19 Teacher check: (example below)
     The colonists did not respect the Indians and took their land without paying for it. The two sides often fought battles which the Indians usually lost.
2.20 Fundamental Orders of Connecticut
2.21 Puritans
2.22 Rhode Island
2.23 John Winthrop
2.24 Roger Williams
2.25 Puritan church members
2.26 Thomas Hooker
2.27 separation of church and state
2.28 Puritans
2.29 Native Americans (Indians)
2.30 c, d
2.31 f
2.32 h
2.33 i
2.34 a
2.35 e
2.36 e
2.37 g
2.38 b
2.39 a
2.40 a
2.41 plantations; slaves
2.42 North Carolina
2.43 Baltimore
2.44 James Oglethorpe; debt
2.45 Catholics
2.46 Virginia
2.47 Georgia
2.48 Toleration

2.49 South Carolina
2.50 tobacco
2.51 indigo

SELF TEST 2

2.01 Jamestown
2.02 Maryland
2.03 Massachusetts
2.04 Virginia
2.05 Connecticut
2.06 Georgia
2.07 Plymouth
2.08 Rhode Island
2.09 New York
2.010 New Jersey
2.011 South Carolina
2.012 Pennsylvania
2.013 Delaware
2.014 New Hampshire
2.015 North Carolina
2.016 b
2.017 f
2.018 c
2.019 d
2.020 g
2.021 h
2.022 i
2.023 a
2.024 j
2.025 e
2.026 charter
2.027 Fundamental Orders of Connecticut
2.028 representative assembly
2.029 proprietor
2.030 spices
2.031 Mayflower Compact
2.032 Puritans
2.033 Pilgrims
2.034 Northwest Passage
2.035 Indentured servants
2.036 true
2.037 false
2.038 true
2.039 true
2.040 true
2.041 false
2.042 true
2.043 false
2.044 true
2.045 true

SECTION 3

3.1 Any order:
   a. governor
   b. council
   c. assembly

3.2 They had to vote for taxes and the governor had to listen to them if he wanted money.

3.3 Very few nobles came to America.

3.4 Men who owned land or a certain amount of money.

3.5 A revival in the 1730s and 40s

3.6 Any order:
   a. Jonathan Edwards
   b. George Whitefield

3.7 the American Revolution

3.8 ignored them

3.9 no

3.10 To make money for Britain and the British people

3.11 the voters

3.12 false

3.13 true

3.14 false

3.15 false

3.16 true

3.17 true

3.18 true

3.19 true

3.20 true

3.21 true

3.22 false

3.23 true

3.24 true

3.25 false

3.26 true

3.27 false

3.28 true

3.29 true

3.30 George Grenville

3.31 Admiralty

3.32 Quartering Act

3.33 Proclamation of 1763

3.34 Sugar Act

3.35 Stamp Act

3.36 Sons of Liberty

3.37 Declaratory Act

3.38 Stamp Act Congress

3.39 Pontiac

3.40 Only an assembly made up of representatives people voted for could tax them.

3.41 They ignored it.

3.42 It was deeply in debt.

3.43 Townshend

3.44 Indians; Tea Party

3.45 Continental Congress

3.46 Boston Massacre

3.47 tea

3.48 boycott; May 1775

3.49 American

3.50 Intolerable

3.51 did not

3.52 Lexington

3.53 They were shot at by Americans from behind trees and such all the way back.

3.54 Paul Revere

3.55 The colonial leaders and war supplies

3.56
   a. Bunker Hill
   b. Breeds Hill

3.57
   a. They voted for independence.
   b. The Declaration of Independence was accepted.

3.58 minutemen

3.59 *Common Sense*

3.60 Thomas Jefferson

3.61 George Washington

3.62 Old North Church

3.63
   a. obvious, does not need to be proven
   b. They are created equal.
   c. life, liberty and the pursuit of happiness
   d. God (their Creator)

SELF TEST 3

3.01   d
3.02   e
3.03   j
3.04   l
3.05   m
3.06   a
3.07   b
3.08   m
3.09   c
3.010 d
3.011 g
3.012 k
3.013 f
3.014 n
3.015 h
3.016 i
3.017 b
3.018 i
3.019 c, e
3.020 m
3.021 Samuel Adams
3.022 Roger Williams
3.023 William Penn
3.024 George III

3.025 George Grenville
3.026 Thomas Jefferson
3.027 Squanto
3.028 William Pitt
3.029 Pontiac
3.030 George Washington
3.031 Virginia (Jamestown)
3.032 He was ambushed by the French and killed.
3.033 boycott
3.034 They had no jury and they were assumed to be guilty.
3.035 Stamp Act Congress
3.036 *Common Sense*
3.037 Any order:
         a. governor
         b. council
         c. assembly
3.038 to make money for Britain and the British people
3.039 false
3.040 true
3.041 true
3.042 true
3.043 false

LIFEPAC TEST

1. d
2. f
3. j
4. e
5. h
6. g
7. i
8. c
9. a
10. b
11. Rhode Island
12. New York
13. North Carolina
14. Plymouth (Massachusetts)
15. Any order:
   a. Pennsylvania
   b. Delaware
16. Massachusetts
17. Connecticut
18. Virginia (Jamestown)
19. South Carolina
20. indentured servants
21. Native Americans (Indians), Asians
22. French and Indian War
23. Intolerable Acts
24. Spain
25. Stamp Act
26. Northwest Passage
27. assembly
28. furs
29. charter
30. a
31. b
32. c
33. b
34. c
35. b
36. a
37. d
38. c
39. b

ALTERNATE LIFEPAC TEST

1. e
2. i
3. n
4. f
5. l
6. m
7. a
8. b
9. k
10. g
11. d
12. j
13. o
14. c
15. h
16. Intolerable Acts
17. Lexington
18. spices
19. Puritans
20. Sons of Liberty
21. Virginia Company of London
22. Native Americans or Indians
23. *Mayflower*
24. French and Indian War
25. Fundamental Orders of Connecticut
26. tobacco
27. Declaration of Independence
28. New Jersey
29. Mississippi
30. Great Awakening
31. Townshend Acts
32. Declaratory Act
33. indentured servants
34. The British marched straight up the hill and were driven back twice with heavy losses. The Americans retreated when they ran out of gunpowder.
35. They met together at the Stamp Act Congress, organized a boycott of British goods and some attacked the people selling the stamps.
36. A governor (elected or appointed) ran most of the government. He was helped by a council he appointed. An assembly elected by the voters raised the taxes.
37. The laws in Massachusetts were strict and only Puritans could vote. Many people left to escape or because they disagreed with how the colony was being run.

HISTORY & GEOGRAPHY 501

ALTERNATE LIFEPAC TEST

NAME _____

DATE _____

SCORE _____

Match these people (each answer, 2 points).

1. _____ Spanish; explored Texas, NM, and Arizona
2. _____ English, sea dog, sailed around the world
3. _____ Catholic, founded Maryland
4. _____ Quaker, founded Delaware
5. _____ 1st European to reach America
6. _____ Native American, helped the colonists at Plymouth
7. _____ Puritan pastor, founded Rhode Island
8. _____ Puritan pastor, founded Connecticut
9. _____ British pastor, evangelist
10. _____ England's "Lost Colony"
11. _____ Explorer for Spain, established the first European colony in the Americas
12. _____ Led a group of kind-hearted men who founded Georgia to help people in debt
13. _____ Took over the land of the Dutch West India Company
14. _____ Commander-in-chief of the American army
15. _____ Explored the Mississippi River for France

a. Roger Williams

b. Thomas Hooker

c. George Washington

d. Columbus

e. Coronado

f. William Penn

g. Roanoke

h. Jolliet

i. Francis Drake

j. James Oglethorpe

k. George Whitefield

l. Leif Ericson

m. Squanto

n. Lord Baltimore

o. Duke of York

Name the law, event, or item (each answer, 3 points).

16. Laws that closed Boston harbor and forbade town meetings _____

17. Battle that began the Revolutionary War _____

18. European explorers wanted to reach Asia to get these _____

19. People who founded Massachusetts to avoid persecution _____

20. Secret group that carried out the Boston Tea Party _____

21. Company that founded Jamestown _____

22. First people to come to North America _____

23. Name of the ship that carried the Pilgrims to Plymouth _____

24. After this war, Britain began to enforce its trade laws and try to control the American colonies _____

25. First constitution in America _____

26. Cash crop for Virginia _____

27. The United States was born when this was accepted by the Second Continental Congress

    _____

28. Colony given by the Duke of York to two friends who eventually sold it to the Quakers

    _____

29. France claimed all the land around this river in the central United States

    _____

30. Revival in America in the 1730s and 1740s _____

31. Laws that put a tax on tea, lead, paint _____

32. Parliament declared it could control the colonies any way it wanted

    _____

33. People who worked for several years in exchange for passage to America

    _____

Answer these questions (each answer, 4 points).

34. Describe what happened at the Battle of Bunker Hill.

    _____

    _____

    _____

35. How did the Americans react to the Stamp Act?

_____

_____

_____

36. How were most colonial governments set up?

_____

_____

_____

37. Why were so many New England colonies started by people from Massachusetts?

_____

_____

_____

HISTORY & GEOGRAPHY 502

Unit 2: A New Nation

TEACHER NOTES

MATERIALS NEEDED FOR LIFEPAC	
Required	Suggested
(None)	• map of the United States

ADDITIONAL LEARNING ACTIVITIES

Section 1: War for Independence

1. Do a class project on one of the battles of the Revolutionary War. Create a model of it. Do reports on the men who fought in it. Explore the Internet by searching these topics: Revolutionary War battles, American Revolution battles, Battle of Bunker Hill, Battle of Lexington and Concord or another specific Revolutionary War battle.

2. Do a written or oral report on the weapons used in the Revolutionary War.

3. Put together a play about the capture and hanging of Nathan Hale.

4. Put together a play about life at Valley Forge.

5. Read about the life of an ordinary soldier in the Revolutionary War. Check your local library or the Internet for information.

6. Learn about Fort Ticonderoga at the library or on the Internet. Make a model of the fort. Explain its importance to the class.

7. Discuss these questions with the class:

   a. Why did the Americans win the Revolutionary War?

   b. What made the Americans fight so long under such bad conditions.

   c. How much did the French help us?

   d. Why would a man like Benedict Arnold betray his country?

   e. What might have happened if the Americans had lost the war?

8. As a class project, learn about some of the less important "Founding Fathers." Learn the names of some of the men who led the Continental Congresses, were generals in the American army and came to the Constitutional Convention. Have each student do a report on one of these men. (This information may be harder than usual to find.)

9. Do a newscast on the progress of the Revolutionary War after a major battle.

Section 2: The Constitution

1. Assign different parts of the Constitution to each student. Have each explain his part to the whole class.

2. Memorize the preamble to the Constitution and recite it to your teacher.

3. Get a copy of the U.S. Constitution and your state Constitution. Compare them in class together.

4. Read a book about the Constitutional Convention.

5. As a class, write a constitution for a government for your school.

6. Hold a class debate on the Constitution. Half the students should be Federalists, the other half Anti-Federalists. Do some research first on what both sides used to support their views.

7. Put on a play about Washington's first cabinet meeting.

8. Have a class discussion on the Bill of Rights. How would life be different in the U.S. if these rights were not protected?

9. Learn about the symbols on the U.S. seal. Report to your class about it.

10. Make a U.S. flag from any time in history. Make sure you know how many stars it should have.

11. Discuss these questions in class:

    a. Why was George Washington a good choice for president?

    b. Do we have taxation without representation today?

    c. What other protections should be added to the Constitution?

    d. Should the Constitutional Convention have compromised on slavery?

    e. What does freedom of speech mean to you? Freedom of religion?

Section 3: A New Republic

1. Do a class project on George Washington. Collect pictures, stories and models about his life to display in your room.

2. Hold a debate over whether or not the National Bank is constitutional. Assign students to play the parts of Jefferson, Hamilton and Washington with other people helping on both sides.

3. Read about the building of Washington, D.C. and report on it to the class.

4. Explore the Internet. Visit the National Park Service website at www.nps.gov, and type "Washington DC" in the site search box. You will discover links to various monuments and historical sites. The world's largest museum and research center—the Smithsonian Institute—is also located in Washington, D.C. Visit www.si.edu to learn more about the Smithsonian.

5. Discuss these questions:

    a. Is it possible for a country to write a constitution detailed enough so that the government can only do what that constitution allows?

    b. What kind of things are "necessary and proper" for the government to do?

    c. Should America have gone to war with France in Europe?

    d. Are political parties good or bad for America?

    e. Who had better ideas, the Federalists or the Democratic-Republicans?

    f. How did the Alien and Sedition Acts violate the Constitution?

    g. Should America have gone to war over the XYZ Affair?

    h. What do the two political parties in America believe today?

6. Read about life on the frontier. Write a report or give a presentation.

7. Write a report or do a presentation on the first cloth making machines.

8. Read a book about whaling.

9. Do a report on slavery in America.

10. Read about how people made things on the frontier, like tools, cloth or furniture. Try to make one item yourself.

Administer the LIFEPAC Test.

The test is to be administered in one session. Give no help except with directions.

Evaluate the tests and review areas where the students have done poorly.

Review the pages and activities that stress the concepts tested.

If necessary, administer the Alternate LIFEPAC Test.

ANSWER KEYS

SECTION 1

1.1   false
1.2   true
1.3   true
1.4   true
1.5   false
1.6   false
1.7   false
1.8   true
1.9   true
1.10 true
1.11 true
1.12 true
1.13 false
1.14 Washington crossed the Delaware R. Christmas night and surprised the Hessian army there. The Americans won and captured 1,000 prisoners.
1.15 Many of the soldiers were ready to give up and go home. They decided to stay and many more came to join because of the victories.
1.16 Nathan Hale
1.17 John Burgoyne
1.18 Howe; St. Leger
1.19 Benjamin Franklin
1.20 Saratoga
1.21 Benedict Arnold
1.22 Valley Forge

1.23 Saratoga
1.24 Philadelphia
1.25 von Steuben
1.26 New York City
1.27 He tried to give the British the fort at West Point in exchange for money and a job.
1.28 John André; he was caught by the Americans and hung as a spy.
1.29 He captured three important forts in the west that stopped the British from giving supplies to the Indians.
1.30 Savannah and Charleston
1.31 The French navy kept the British from reaching Cornwallis while Washington and Rochambeau laid siege to the British camp and it surrendered.
1.32 He made them chase him all over until their supplies and men were exhausted.
1.33 a.   east of the Mississippi between Canada and Florida
         b.   pay their debts and try to return things taken from the Tories
1.34 yes
1.35 A French general who came to America with an army to help us
1.36 eight years

SELF TEST 1

1.01	b
1.02	e
1.03	a
1.04	c
1.05	d
1.06	k
1.07	g
1.08	i
1.09	f
1.010	j
1.011	h
1.012	l
1.013	France
1.014	a. Lexington
	b. Yorktown
1.015	Tories
1.016	Ticonderoga
1.017	Saratoga
1.018	Valley Forge
1.019	Hessians
1.020	Second Continental Congress
1.021	Philadelphia
1.022	Indians
1.023	true
1.024	false
1.025	false
1.026	false
1.027	false
1.028	true
1.029	false
1.030	true
1.031	false
1.032	true

SECTION 2

2.1	
2.2	X
2.3	X
2.4	
2.5	X
2.6	X
2.7	X
2.8	
2.9	c
2.10	d
2.11	b
2.12	a
2.13	e
2.14	Any order:
	a. George Washington, Virginia
	b. Benjamin Franklin, Pennsylvania
	c. Alexander Hamilton, New York
	d. James Madison, Virginia
2.15	Teacher check
2.16	Any order: legislative, executive, judicial
2.17	nine or two-thirds of the
2.18	Virginia
2.19	New Jersey
2.20	Senate; House of Representatives
2.21	Connecticut
2.22	Three-fifths
2.23	1808
2.24	two-thirds
2.25	control
2.26	Federalists
2.27	Anti-Federalists
2.28	Any order: James Madison, John Jay, Alexander Hamilton
2.29	Delaware
2.30	New Hampshire
2.31	a. It did not protect the freedoms of the people
	b. They promised that the first Congress would add Amendments to do that.
2.32	a. Thomas Jefferson
	b. Alexander Hamilton
	c. Henry Knox
	d. Edmund Randolf
2.33	George Washington
2.34	Bill of Rights
2.35	thirteen
2.36	states
2.37	bald eagle
2.38	*E Pluribus Unum*
2.39	First
2.40	New York City

SELF TEST 2

2.01 c
2.02 g
2.03 a
2.04 d
2.05 i
2.06 j
2.07 b
2.08 e
2.09 h
2.010 f
2.011 George Washington
2.012 Any order: judicial (courts), executive (president), legislative (Congress)
2.013 Lexington
2.014 bald eagle
2.015 First
2.016 two-thirds
2.017 France
2.018 Mississippi
2.019 George Rogers Clark
2.020 Benjamin Franklin
2.021 James Madison
2.022 Nathan Hale
2.023 Baron von Stuben
2.024 Thomas Jefferson
2.025 Nathanael Greene
2.026 Alexander Hamilton
2.027 George Washington
2.028 Benedict Arnold
2.029 true
2.030 false
2.031 false
2.032 false
2.033 true
2.034 false
2.035 false
2.036 false
2.037 true
2.038 true

SECTION 3

3.1 none
3.2 a National Bank
3.3 The south agreed to let the federal government take over the state debts if family the capital was put in the South.
3.4 Whiskey Rebellion
3.5 First Lady
3.6 Washington, District of Columbia
3.7 debt
3.8 only things it listed as allowable
3.9 tariffs and whiskey taxes
3.10 "necessary and proper"
3.11 a.   f. X
       b. X   g. X
       c.   h.
       d. X   i
       e. X
3.12 a. X
       b.
       c. X
       d. X
       e.
3.13 a. X
       b.
       c.
3.14 a. X   g.
       b. X   h.
       c. X   i. X
       d. X
       e.
       f.
3.15 cotton gin
3.16 rum; slaves; molasses
3.17 land; slaves
3.18 more
3.19 Middle
3.20 easier
3.21 a. George Washington
       b. John Adams
       c. Thomas Jefferson
3.22 a. Thomas Jefferson
       b. Alexander Hamilton
3.23 none
3.24 XYZ Affair
3.25 Alien and Sedition
3.26 White House
3.27 Any order:
       a. He did not go to war with France.
       b. The Alien and Sedition Acts
3.28 Pierre Charles L'Enfant
3.29 two

SELF TEST 3

3.01   h
3.02   i
3.03   j
3.04   f
3.05   b
3.06   g
3.07   c
3.08   d
3.09   e
3.010 a
3.011 Washington, D.C.
3.012 XYZ
3.013 two
3.014 Middle
3.015 Lexington; Yorktown
3.016 Any order: judicial (courts), executive (president), legislative (congress)
3.017 New England
3.018 Northwest Ordinance
3.019 Democratic-Republican
3.020 First Amendment
3.021 Hessians
3.022 Bill of Rights
3.023 circuit riders
3.024 Articles of Confederation

3.025 Great Compromise
3.026 Whiskey Rebellion
3.027 Alien and Sedition Acts
3.028 Valley Forge
3.029 Tories
3.030 a.
          b.
          c.
          d. X
          e.
3.031 a.
          b.
          c. X
          d.
          e. X
3.032 a. X
          b.
          c. X
          d. X
          e.
3.033 a.
          b.
          c. X
          d. X
          e. X

LIFEPAC TEST

1. cotton gin
2. Yorktown
3. Bill of Rights
4. Senate; Representatives
5. France
6. Northwest
7. Saratoga
8. Federalists
9. Valley Forge
10. c
11. b
12. a
13. c
14. c
15. c
16. a
17. d
18. c
19. b
20. true
21. false
22. true
23. false
24. false
25. false
26. true
27. false
28. true
29. false
30. f
31. h
32. g
33. b
34. a
35. i
36. d
37. j
38. e
39. c

ALTERNATE LIFEPAC TEST

1. p
2. h
3. n
4. r
5. o
6. t
7. s
8. l
9. m
10. b
11. a
12. e
13. j
14. c
15. k
16. i
17. d
18. q
19. f
20. g
21. Any order: judicial (courts), executive (president), legislative (congress)
22. The U.S. was an ally of France, but Washington decided to stay neutral.
23. a. He was afraid it was not legal because the Constitution says nothing about a bank.
    b. Hamilton convinced him that it was allowed as "necessary and proper" under the Constitution.
24. Any order:
    a. Democratic-Republicans
    b. Federalists
25. interchangeable parts
26. The cotton gin made it easy to clean and the new cloth factories needed it.
27. Any order: molasses, rum, slaves
28. The south agreed to let the national government take the state debts if it was put there.
29. true
30. true
31. false
32. false
33. false
34. false
35. true
36. true
37. true
38. true
39. b
40. i
41. f

42. j
43. c
44. e
45. h
46. a
47. d
48. g

HISTORY & GEOGRAPHY 502

ALTERNATE LIFEPAC TEST

NAME _____

DATE _____

SCORE _____

Match these items (each answer, 2 points).

1. _____ After the war, it gave America the land east of the Mississippi

2. _____ Area famous for fishing, whaling, and shipbuilding

3. _____ Fort taken by the Green Mountain Boys, its cannons were used at Boston

4. _____ Tax revolt in Pennsylvania, stopped by Washington

5. _____ People who did not want the Constitution

6. _____ Has an eagle holding arrows and an olive branch

7. _____ People who advise and assist the president

8. _____ Americans captured Burgoyne's army, made the French decide to join us as allies

9. _____ Washington crossed the Delaware on Christmas night and took his enemies by surprise

10. _____ German soldiers paid to fight for the British

11. _____ U.S. government that had no president, no courts and Congress could not tax

12. _____ A territory could become a state when it had 60,000 people

13. _____ Part of the slave trade when captives were jammed into a ship for the trip to the Americas

14. _____ The Constitutional Convention agreed to divide Congress into the Senate and the House of Representatives

15. _____ Last major battle of the war, Washington and Rochambeau trapped a British army after the French navy stopped the British navy from reaching them

16. _____ Area of poor, independent farmers who were far from towns and had circuit riders for pastors

17. _____ First ten Amendments to the Constitution, protects our freedoms

18. _____ The French refused to talk without a bribe, almost started a war

19. _____ Divided the Northwest Territory into townships of 36 sections for sale

a. Articles of Confederation

b. Hessians

c. Great Compromise

d. Bill of Rights

e. Northwest Ordinance

f. Land Ordinance (1785)

g. Alien and Sedition Acts

h. New England

i. Frontier

j. Middle Passage

k. Yorktown

l. Saratoga

m. Trenton

n. Ticonderoga

o. Anti-Federalists

p. Treaty of Paris

q. XYZ Affair

r. Whiskey Rebellion

s. Cabinet

t. Great Seal of the U.S.

20. _____ Law that forbade saying bad things about the government and made it more difficult for people to become citizens

Answer these questions (each answer, 3 points).

21. What are the three branches of the U.S. government? _____

_____

22. Why did the war in Europe pose a problem for President Washington and what did he do?

_____

23. Why did President Washington hesitate to sign the law creating a National Bank?

a. _____

_____

Why did he sign it?

b. _____

_____

24. What were America's first two political parties?

a. _____

b. _____

25. What did Eli Whitney use that made gun making easier?

_____

26. Why did the south start growing so much cotton?_____

_____

27. What were the three main items in the triangle trade between America, the West Indies, and Africa? _____

28. Why was the U.S. capital put in the south? _____

_____

Write *true* or *false* (each answer, 1 point).

29. _____ George Washington was chosen to lead the Constitutional Convention.

30. _____ Americans loyal to Britain during the Revolution were called Tories.

31. _____ The Americans refused to repay their debts to Britain after the Revolution.

32. _____ The Confederation Congress accomplished nothing good.

33. _____ One-half of the states must agree to add an Amendment to the Constitution.

34. _____ American manufacturing began in the South.

35. _____ George Washington was not a member of any political party.

36. _____ John Adams was the second president of the United States.

37. _____ Alexander Hamilton wrote essays in favor of the Constitution.

38. _____ The British had to conquer all of America to win the Revolutionary War.

Match these people (each answer, 2 points).

39. _____ "Father of the Constitution"

40. _____ Captured important forts in the West

41. _____ Inventor, printer from Philadelphia

42. _____ First vice president

43. _____ Captured Fort Ticonderoga

44. _____ Cleared the British out of the South, losing all the battles

45. _____ Started the first cloth factory in America

46. _____ Third president of the U.S.

47. _____ Drilled the American army at Valley Forge

48. _____ Hero at Saratoga, turned traitor

a. Thomas Jefferson

b. James Madison

c. Ethan Allen

d. Baron von Steuben

e. Nathanael Greene

f. Benjamin Franklin

g. Benedict Arnold

h. Samuel Slater

i. George Rogers Clark

j. John Adams

HISTORY & GEOGRAPHY 503

Unit 3: A Time for Testing

TEACHER NOTES

MATERIALS NEEDED FOR LIFEPAC	
Required	Suggested
(None)	• map of the United States

ADDITIONAL LEARNING ACTIVITIES

Section 1: Jefferson

1. Make a map of the Louisiana Purchase showing how many states were made from that land.

2. Explore the Internet by searching "Thomas Jefferson." Write a paper about his life. (Teacher's warning: Some of the Jefferson sites discuss the gossip about Jefferson's slave girl, Sally Hemmings, who allegedly had several children by him.)

3. Discuss the beliefs of Thomas Jefferson about government. Were they good or bad ideas?

4. Read a book and/or do a report about the Lewis and Clark Expedition. Check out www.lewisandclark.org for information.

5. Do a class play about the Lewis and Clark Expedition.

6. Explore the Internet by searching these topics: Lewis and Clark and Lewis and Clark Expedition. Report your discoveries to the class.

7. Read about the navy's battles with the Barbary pirates.

8. Research and do a paper or report on the Tecumseh Confederacy.

9. Read a book about the Napoleonic Wars in Europe.

10. Build a model of a log cabin.

11. Read a fiction story about life on the frontier.

12. Discuss these questions in class:

    a. What could have been done to stop impressment?

    b. Why was the Lewis and Clark Expedition so important?

    c. What would it have been like to go on the Lewis and Clark Expedition?

    d. How would you feel if you lived in 1807 and heard about the *Chesapeake* incident?

Section 2: War of 1812

1. Discuss these questions in class:

    a. What should the U.S. have done to get ready for war?

    b. Was the invasion of Canada a good idea?

    c. Were tariffs a good idea?

  d. How would America be different if the British had won the War of 1812?

2. Make a model or diagram of the Battle of Lake Erie or New Orleans.

3. Explore the Internet by searching "War of 1812." Bookmark your favorite sites, and revisit them to help you complete assigned activities.

4. Explore the Internet for information about the U.S.S. *Constitution*, and find out what made this U.S. Navy ship famous. Do an Internet search for "history of the Star Spangled Banner," and discover what inspired the United States' national anthem.

5. Do a report on the ship to ship battles of the War of 1812, the Battle of New Orleans, the Battle of Lake Erie, the Battle of Baltimore, the burning of Washington or weapons used in the War of 1812.

6. As a class read and discuss the words to the "Star Spangled Banner."

Section 3: Changes After the War

1. Write a report on the life of Henry Clay, John Quincy Adams, James Monroe or James Madison.

2. Discuss the Missouri Compromise in class:

  a. Was it a fair compromise?

  b. Did it solve the problem?

  c. What could go wrong with it?

  d. Should the North have compromised on slavery?

3. Choose people in the class to pretend to be from the North, South and West. Have each defend their opinions on slavery in the territories, the tariff, government built roads and land prices.

4. Read about the four men who ran for president in 1824. Then, pretend your class is the House of Representatives and vote on who will be president.

5. Do a paper or report on the Erie Canal, steamboats, the National Road or St. Louis as a frontier town.

6. Explore the Internet. Do a search for "Erie Canal" to learn about the history and construction of the canal. Visit the website of the Erie Canal Village (www.eriecanalvillage.com) to discover this living history museum of a reconstructed Erie Canal settlement. Search the Internet on the "history of steamboats" or "steamboats in American history" to learn how this invention impacted U.S. history.

7. Make a map or model of the Erie Canal.

8. Read about the history of Florida before it was part of the United States. Give a report to the class.

9. Research the beliefs of the Democratic and Whig political parties in the 1820s and 30s. Make a chart showing the differences.

Administer the LIFEPAC Test.

ANSWER KEYS

SECTION 1

1.1	
1.2	X
1.3	
1.4	X
1.5	X
1.6	
1.7	X
1.8	
1.9	X
1.10	Louisiana; 15 million
1.11	Any order: Meriwether Lewis, William Clark; Columbia; Pacific
1.12	Sacagawea; Lewis and Clark
1.13	Tripoli
1.14	ransom
1.15	Any order: Tippecanoe, William Henry Harrison
1.16	22
1.17	$320
1.18	pioneers
1.19	log cabin
1.20	Any order: Fallen Timbers, Mad Anthony Wayne
1.21	Tecumseh
1.22	Vermont
1.23	Britain
1.24	War Hawks
1.25	an embargo
1.26	James Madison
1.27	impressment
1.28	They kept forts in the Northwest, were giving guns to the Indians, seizing U.S. cargoes and impressing sailors.
1.29	O-grab-me
1.30	New England
1.31	Any order: War of 1812, Second War for Independence
1.32	Canada
1.33	U.S.S. *Chesapeake*

SELF TEST 1

1.01	b
1.02	a
1.03	d
1.04	f
1.05	b
1.06	h
1.07	e
1.08	c
1.09	g
1.010	a
1.011	Lewis and Clark
1.012	Barbary or North African
1.013	pioneers
1.014	British
1.015	embargo
1.016	War Hawks
1.017	War of 1812
1.018	log cabins
1.019	Louisiana Purchase
1.020	impressment
1.021	false
1.022	true
1.023	true
1.024	false
1.025	true
1.026	false
1.027	false
1.028	false
1.029	true
1.030	true

SECTION 2

2.1	U.S.S. *Constitution*
2.2	Lake Erie
2.3	Canada
2.4	Detroit
2.5	Oliver Perry
2.6	thirteen
2.7	blockade
2.8	William Henry Harrison
2.9	Tories
2.10	taxes
2.11	Any order: Lake Erie, Plattsburg Bay
2.12	Washington, D.C.
2.13	Thomas Mcdonough
2.14	Any order: Chippewa, Lundy's Lane
2.15	Maine
2.16	Francis Scott Key
2.17	Fort McHenry
2.18	Dolley Madison
2.19	Indians
2.20	Treaty of Ghent
2.21	Andrew Jackson
2.22	Horseshoe Bend
2.23	The U.S. won at Plattsburg Bay and Baltimore. Britain knew it would be a long fight and they were tired of war.
2.24	He was slashed by a British soldier during the Revolution for refusing to clean his boots.
2.25	Any order: manufacturing, nationalism
2.26	They raised the price of foreign goods so people bought the American ones.
2.27	It was fought after the war had ended.
2.28	a. northeast b. west and south
2.29	Old Hickory

SELF TEST 2

2.01	g
2.02	j
2.03	c
2.04	e
2.05	d
2.06	i
2.07	h
2.08	b
2.09	a
2.010	f
2.011	The Democratic-Republican Congress had not raised money to expand the tiny navy and army.
2.012	The Tories who fled the U.S. during the Revolution and the Frenchmen of New France.
2.013	The Constitution did not allow land purchases but it was too good to pass up.
2.014	They were sick of war and the U.S. had won enough that it would be a long war to continue.
2.015	It was fought after the war was finished.
2.016	It raised the prices of foreign goods so that people bought the American ones.
2.017	They burned most of the public buildings.
2.018	The British would stop a U.S. ship and take some of the sailors to serve in their navy.
2.019	An invasion of N.Y. down Lake Champlain.
2.020	Land west of the Mississippi bought by the U.S. from France in 1803.
2.021	nationalism; manufacturing
2.022	Fallen Timbers
2.023	*Chesapeake*
2.024	War Hawks
2.025	pioneers
2.026	*Constitution*
2.027	Treaty of Ghent
2.028	Horseshoe Bend
2.029	embargo
2.030	true
2.031	true
2.032	true
2.033	false
2.034	true
2.035	false
2.036	true
2.037	true
2.038	true

SECTION 3

3.1	a.	X
	b.	X
	c.	
	d.	
	e.	
	f.	
	g.	X
3.2	a.	X
	b.	
	c.	
	d.	X
	e.	X
3.3	a.	
	b.	X
	c.	
	d.	X
	e.	
	f.	X
3.4	a.	
	b.	X
	c.	X
	d.	X
	e.	
3.5	a.	
	b.	X
	c.	X
	d.	X
	e.	X
3.6	N	
3.7	S, W	
3.8	N	

3.9 W
3.10 N
3.11 S
3.12 W
3.13 S, N
3.14 Many of them became independent republics.
3.15 The nations of Europe could not take any more colonies in the Americas. If they did, the U.S. would react as if they were threatening us.
3.16 tariffs and slavery
3.17 The election was decided in the House of Representatives. Henry Clay, who was the Speaker, supported John Quincy Adams, who won.
3.18 Democrat and Whig
3.19 Cumberland
3.20 St. Louis
3.21 turnpikes
3.22 Robert Fulton
3.23 *Clermont*; Fulton's Folly
3.24 Erie Canal; Clinton's Ditch
3.25 Lancaster Turnpike
3.26 Erie; Mohawk or Hudson
3.27 DeWitt Clinton
3.28 steamboat
3.29 Baltimore; St. Louis

SELF TEST 3

3.01	j	**3.021**	Democrat
3.02	d	**3.022**	Whig
3.03	g	**3.023**	Tecumseh Confederacy
3.04	b	**3.024**	Impressment
3.05	e	**3.025**	Adams-Onis Treaty
3.06	h	**3.026**	American System
3.07	f	**3.027**	Plattsburg Bay
3.08	a	**3.028**	Treaty of Ghent
3.09	c	**3.029**	Barbary Coast
3.010	i	**3.030**	Embargo
3.011	Lewis and Clark	**3.031**	true
3.012	Erie	**3.032**	true
3.013	National or Cumberland	**3.033**	true
3.014	Democratic-Republican	**3.034**	false
3.015	Missouri	**3.035**	true
3.016	Monroe	**3.036**	true
3.017	turnpikes	**3.037**	true
3.018	War for Independence	**3.038**	true
3.019	"Star Spangled Banner"	**3.039**	false
3.020	Maine	**3.040**	true

LIFEPAC TEST

1. e
2. j
3. h
4. a
5. c
6. b
7. g
8. i
9. d
10. f
11. true
12. false
13. false
14. true
15. false
16. The British were taking U.S. cargoes, impressing U.S. sailors, holding forts in the Northwest Territory and giving guns to the Indians there.
17. f
18. k
19. m
20. n
21. q
22. p
23. b
24. o
25. c
26. r
27. s
28. a
29. d
30. g
31. h
32. e
33. t
34. j
35. i
36. l
37. nationalism; sectionalism
38. tariff
39. embargo
40. pioneers
41. Impressment
42. War for Independence
43. Steamboats
44. Erie
45. Democratic

ALTERNATE LIFEPAC TEST

1. f
2. a
3. m
4. l
5. a
6. h
7. b
8. g
9. j
10. j
11. c
12. k
13. e
14. d
15. i
16. a
17. f
18. a
19. m
20. l
21. Monroe
22. Louisiana Purchase
23. manufacturing
24. War Hawks
25. Canada
26. Erie
27. Missouri
28. Democratic-Republican
29. Florida
30. Constitution
31. Because Britain was impressing U.S. sailors, seizing U.S. ships, holding forts in U.S. territory and giving guns to the Indians
32. The North wanted high tariffs, high land prices and no slavery in the territories. The South wanted low tariffs and slavery in the territories. The West wanted low land prices and low tariffs.

HISTORY & GEOGRAPHY 503

ALTERNATE LIFEPAC TEST

NAME _____

DATE _____

SCORE _____

Match these people. Some answers will be used more than once (each answer, 3 points).

1. _____ President, asked for war with Britain in 1812
2. _____ Sent out the Lewis and Clark Expedition
3. _____ Speaker of the House
4. _____ Wrote the "Star Spangled Banner"
5. _____ Sent the U.S. Navy to fight the pirates of Tripoli
6. _____ Invented the steamboat
7. _____ Won the presidency in the House of Representatives with Henry Clay's help
8. _____ Ran for president unopposed
9. _____ Won the Battle of New Orleans
10. _____ Attacked the Indians in Florida and captured two important outposts there
11. _____ Created an alliance among the Mississippi R. Indians
12. _____ Won the Battle of Fallen Timbers against the Indians of the Northwest Territory
13. _____ "We have met the enemy and they are ours."
14. _____ Led the Indiana militia to defeat an Indian alliance at the Battle of Tippecanoe
15. _____ Governor of New York, built a successful canal
16. _____ Bought land from France even though he did not believe the Constitution allowed him to do it
17. _____ His wife saved many of the White House treasures from the British
18. _____ Tried to hurt the British and French with an embargo but only hurt Americans
19. _____ The Great Compromiser
20. _____ Watched the bombardment of Fort McHenry from a British ship

a. Thomas Jefferson
b. John Quincy Adams
c. Tecumseh
d. William Henry Harrison
e. Oliver Perry
f. James Madison
g. James Monroe
h. Robert Fulton
i. DeWitt Clinton
j. Andrew Jackson
k. Mad Anthony Wayne
l. Francis Scott Key
m. Henry Clay

Complete these sentences (each answer, 3 points).

21. The _____ Doctrine said that European countries could no longer take colonies in the Americas.

22. The _____ was land America bought from France west of the Mississippi River in 1803.

23. The War of 1812 resulted in an increase in nationalism in the whole country and

    _____ in the northeast.

24. The _____ were young Congressmen from the South and West

    that wanted war with Britain.

25. The United States immediately invaded the country of _____ after declaring

    war in 1812.

26. The _____ Canal connected the Great Lakes to the Atlantic Ocean.

27. The _____ Compromise forbade slavery north of a line at 36°30' in

    the U.S. territories.

28. The _____ Party was the only powerful political party after the

    War of 1812.

29. The state of _____ was added to the U.S. in the

    Adams-Onis Treaty with Spain.

30. The most famous U.S. ship of the War of 1812 was the U.S.S. _____ .

Answer these questions (each answer, 5 points).

31. Why did America go to war with Britain in 1812? _____

    _____

    _____

    _____

32. What did the North, South, and West want for tariffs, slavery, and land prices (when they had

    an opinion)? _____

    _____

    _____

    _____

    _____

HISTORY & GEOGRAPHY 504

Unit 4: A Growing Nation

TEACHER NOTES

MATERIALS NEEDED FOR LIFEPAC	
Required	Suggested
(None)	• map of the United States

ADDITIONAL LEARNING ACTIVITIES

Section 1: The Time of Jackson

1. Do a one-page story of the life of Andrew Jackson, Martin Van Buren, William Henry Harrison, John Tyler, Daniel Webster or James Polk

2. Discuss these questions in class:

    a. Why was the Spoils System bad?

    b. Why was Andrew Jackson so different from the presidents before him?

    c. What was good and bad about Manifest Destiny?

    d. If you were an eastern Indian, would you have fought or moved in 1830?

    e. Why was nullification such a serious issue?

    f. How would you feel if you were an eastern Indian forced to leave on the Trail of Tears?

3. Stage your own Webster-Hayne Debate after discussing arguments for and against nullification.

4. Explore the Internet by searching these topics: Andrew Jackson and Trail of Tears.

Section 2: Manifest Destiny

1. Do a report on any of these topics: the Texas Revolution, the Oregon Trail, the Mexican War, Railroads in the 1830s-1860s, the Second Great Awakening, Irish Immigration to America during the Potato Famine or the Telegraph.

2. Do an oral report or written paper on one of these men: Sam Houston, Stephen Austin, Davy Crockett, William Travis, Jim Bowie, Santa Anna, Zachary Taylor, Winfield Scott, Samuel Morse, Cyrus McCormick or John Deere.

3. As a class pretend to be pioneers, research and plan a trip on the Oregon Trail. Choose what you will take, when you will go and where you will settle.

4. Discuss these questions in class:

    a. Should Andrew Jackson have immediately admitted Texas to the Union?

    b. What if Texas had stayed as a republic until today?

  c. Why would people have risked the dangers of the Oregon Trail?

  d. What do you think about James Polk starting a war by sending troops south of the Nueces River?

  e. Was the Treaty of Guadalupe-Hidalgo fair?

  f. Why was the telegraph such an important invention?

5. Build a model of the Alamo.

6. Read a fiction book about pioneers traveling the Oregon Trail or living through the Texas Revolution.

7. Explore the Internet by searching these topics: American West, Oregon Trail and Whitman Mission.

Section 3: Dividing the Nation

1. Do a biography on one of these people: Stephen Douglas, John Brown, Abraham Lincoln or Harriet Tubman.

2. Do a written or oral report on any of these subjects: the California Gold Rush, Bleeding Kansas, the Underground Railroad, the Dred Scott Case, the Fugitive Slave Act, Abolition in America, or John Brown's Raid on Harpers Ferry.

3. Learn how to pan for gold. Build models of some of the equipment used by prospectors.

4. Read a true or fiction story about someone who escaped on the Underground Railroad. Discuss in class what such an escape would have been like.

5. Discuss these questions in class:

  a. Was Henry Clay right or wrong to keep compromising?

  b. Would you have helped in the Underground Railroad knowing you could lose everything you own or go to jail?

  c. Would you have gone to California to find gold?

  d. Why did things get so out of hand in Kansas?

  e. Did the south really need slaves? Why or why not?

6. Do a one act play on a scene from *Uncle Tom's Cabin*.

7. Stage your own Lincoln-Douglas Debates.

8. Explore the Internet by searching these topics: California gold rush and Underground Railroad.

Administer the LIFEPAC Test.

The test is to be administered in one session. Give no help except with directions.

Evaluate the tests and review areas where the students have done poorly.

Review the pages and activities that stress the concepts tested.

If necessary, administer the Alternate LIFEPAC Test.

ANSWER KEYS

SECTION 1

1.1	He was born poor, came from the West, vetoed more laws than all the presidents before him.
1.2	Spoils System
1.3	Old Hickory
1.4	vetoed it
1.5	pet banks
1.6	inauguration
1.7	ordinary people
1.8	Any order: Robert Hayne, Daniel Webster
1.9	nullification
1.10	Daniel Webster
1.11	South Carolina
1.12	Henry Clay
1.13	Trail of Tears
1.14	Andrew Jackson
1.15	Black Hawk
1.16	Seminole
1.17	Andrew Jackson
1.18	reduce; withdraw
1.19	Webster-Hayne
1.20	William Henry Harrison
1.21	William Henry Harrison
1.22	Martin Van Buren
1.23	Martin Van Buren
1.24	James Polk
1.25	Martin Van Buren
1.26	Andrew Jackson
1.27	John Tyler
1.28	William Henry Harrison
1.29	John Tyler
1.30	John Tyler
1.31	James Polk

1.32

ACROSS	DOWN
4. Polk	1. Clay
5. Tyler	2. Harrison
6. Webster	3. Van Buren
7. Jackson	

SELF TEST 1

1.01	e
1.02	f
1.03	a. f
	b. e (either order)
1.04	g
1.05	f
1.06	a
1.07	a
1.08	a
1.09	g
1.010	b
1.011	c
1.012	f
1.013	d
1.014	d
1.015	e
1.016	Manifest
1.017	Spoils
1.018	Nullification
1.019	National Bank
1.020	Webster-Hayne
1.021	Tears
1.022	pet
1.023	vetoed
1.024	Seminole
1.025	Depression
1.026	true
1.027	false
1.028	true
1.029	true
1.030	true
1.031	true

SECTION 2

2.1	Lone Star Republic	**2.33**	Mexican Cession
2.2	Santa Anna	**2.34**	$15 million
2.3	Alamo	**2.35**	Nueces
2.4	San Jacinto	**2.36**	Rio Grande
2.5	Stephen Austin	**2.37**	Buena Vista
2.6	Sam Houston	**2.38**	a. Samuel Morse
2.7	Davy Crockett		b. John Deere
2.8	Jim Bowie		c. Cyrus McCormick
2.9	1845	**2.39**	Morse Code
2.10	The Mexicans killed all of the men who fought so bravely to defend it.	**2.40**	"What hath God wrought?"
2.11	Mexico threatened war and the North did not want to add so much slave territory.	**2.41**	Any order: Germany, Ireland
		2.42	A cable across the Atlantic Ocean
2.12	Polk made it a campaign issue and it was annexed when he won.	**2.43**	The horse won.
		2.44	Second Great Awakening
2.13	false	**2.45**	the push to end slavery
2.14	false	**2.46**	a. manufactured goods
2.15	true		b. cotton
2.16	true		c. food
2.17	false	**2.47**	Potato Famine
2.18	false	**2.48**	camp meetings
2.19	false	**2.49**	It could carry large cargoes places where there were no rivers or canals.
2.20	true		
2.21	true	**2.50**	a. 13
2.22	false		b. 30,000
2.23	true	**2.51**	F
2.24	James Polk	**2.52**	B
2.25	Zachary Taylor	**2.53**	D
2.26	Stephen Kearny	**2.54**	G
2.27	Winfield Scott	**2.55**	C
2.28	Zachary Taylor	**2.56**	A
2.29	Santa Anna	**2.57**	E
2.30	Zachary Taylor		
2.31	Winfield Scott		
2.32	Gadsden Purchase		

SELF TEST 2

2.01	g
2.02	i
2.03	h
2.04	c
2.05	a
2.06	j
2.07	f
2.08	d
2.09	b
2.010	e
2.011	Alamo
2.012	Manifest Destiny
2.013	"Fifty-four Forty or Fight!"
2.014	Spoils
2.015	Mexican Cession
2.016	The horse
2.017	Potato Famine
2.018	Second Great
2.019	Rio Grande
2.020	Nullification
2.021	E
2.022	D
2.023	A
2.024	F
2.025	B
2.026	G
2.027	C
2.028	true
2.029	true
2.030	false
2.031	true
2.032	true
2.033	true
2.034	false
2.035	true
2.036	true
2.037	true
2.038	true

SECTION 3

3.1	California was admitted as a free state; Fugitive Slave Act passed
3.2	Henry Clay
3.3	Sutter's Mill
3.4	Underground Railroad
3.5	Harriet Tubman
3.6	They could not post bail, testify for themselves or have a jury hear their case.
3.7	Forty-niners
3.8	They were fined or put in jail.
3.9	Thousands of people came in the gold rush and stayed to live.
3.10	an equal vote in the Senate (giving the North control of Congress)
3.11	*Uncle Tom's Cabin*
3.12	Kansas-Nebraska
3.13	abolitionists
3.14	Bleeding Kansas
3.15	Harriet Beecher Stowe
3.16	*The Liberator*
3.17	spreading
3.18	Republican
3.19	God
3.20	John Brown
3.21	Dred Scott
3.22	Honest Abe
3.23	Lincoln-Douglas Debates
3.24	That slaves were property protected by the Constitution and, therefore, slavery was legal in all of the United States.
3.25	a. Kentucky b. Indiana c. Illinois
3.26	Republican
3.27	Five of the nine justices were from the South.
3.28	They protested, made a song about him and hailed him as a martyr.
3.29	Stephen Douglas
3.30	South Carolina
3.31	It was wrong. It should not be allowed to spread. However, the federal government did not have the power to stop it in the South.
3.32	The election of Lincoln
3.33	The Confederate States of America; Jefferson Davis

SELF TEST 3

3.01	b	**3.021**	c
3.02	h	**3.022**	b
3.03	j	**3.023**	c
3.04	g	**3.024**	a
3.05	a	**3.025**	a
3.06	i	**3.026**	b
3.07	c	**3.027**	d
3.08	e	**3.028**	b
3.09	f	**3.029**	d
3.010	d	**3.030**	d
3.011	gold rush	**3.031**	true
3.012	Underground Railroad	**3.032**	false
3.013	*Uncle Tom's Cabin*	**3.033**	true
3.014	Kansas-Nebraska Act	**3.034**	false
3.015	Potato Famine	**3.035**	false
3.016	Bleeding Kansas	**3.036**	false
3.017	Lincoln-Douglas Debates	**3.037**	false
3.018	Alamo	**3.038**	false
3.019	Compromise of 1850	**3.039**	true
3.020	Dred Scott Decision	**3.040**	true

LIFEPAC TEST

1. C
2. E
3. D
4. F
5. G
6. c
7. b
8. a
9. b
10. a
11. i
12. h
13. j
14. g
15. c
16. a
17. f
18. b
19. d
20. e
21. Manifest Destiny
22. Oregon
23. Webster-Hayne
24. *Uncle Tom's Cabin*
25. Compromise of 1850
26. Sutter's Mill
27. Oregon Trail
28. Trail of Tears
29. Dred Scott
30. Underground Railroad
31. false
32. true
33. true
34. true
35. true
36. false
37. false
38. true
39. true
40. true

ALTERNATE LIFEPAC TEST

1. r
2. v
3. n
4. g
5. k
6. q
7. l
8. x
9. t
10. f
11. s
12. a
13. m
14. o
15. u
16. w
17. b
18. e
19. p
20. y
21. j
22. c
23. i
24. h
25. d
26. h
27. j
28. c
29. n
30. l
31. g
32. o
33. i
34. d
35. e
36. k
37. m
38. f
39. a
40. b
41. false
42. false
43. true
44. false
45. true
46. false
47. true
48. false
49. true
50. true

HISTORY & GEOGRAPHY 504

ALTERNATE LIFEPAC TEST

NAME _____

DATE _____

SCORE _____

Choose the correct letter (each answer, 2 points).

1. _____ Allowed territories to choose slavery or not

2. _____ Debate over nullification

3. _____ Revival in the early 1800s

4. _____ Removal of Indians east of the Mississippi

5. _____ Largest piece of land added to the U.S.

6. _____ Group that helped slaves escape

7. _____ Caused Irish to come to America

8. _____ First state to secede from the Union

9. _____ Popular abolitionist book

10. _____ Jackson vetoed it; put federal money in pet banks

11. _____ Gold found in California

12. _____ Government jobs went to the president's supporters

13. _____ Mexico claimed this was the border of Texas

14. _____ 2,000-mile route to Oregon from Missouri

15. _____ Debate over slavery in an Illinois election

16. _____ State that rebelled against Mexico, was a republic

17. _____ California admitted, Fugitive Slave Act passed

18. _____ South Carolina refused to obey the tariff

19. _____ Railroad engine that lost a race with a horse

20. _____ James Polk sent American soldiers into disputed territory to start this to get California

21. _____ Land wanted in "Fifty-four Forty or Fight!"

22. _____ Supreme Court said slavery was legal in all America

23. _____ Mission in which all the defenders were killed

24. _____ Attack on the arsenal at Harpers Ferry to start a slave revolt

25. _____ America was to spread across the continent

a. Spoils System

b. Compromise of 1850

c. Dred Scott Decision

d. Manifest Destiny

e. Nullification Crisis

f. National Bank

g. Trail of Tears

h. John Brown's Raid

i. Alamo

j. Oregon Country

k. Mexican Cession

l. Potato Famine

m. Nueces River

n. Second Great Awakening

o. Oregon Trail

p. *Tom Thumb*

q. Underground Railroad

r. Kansas-Nebraska Act

s. Sutter's Mill

t. *Uncle Tom's Cabin*

u. Lincoln-Douglas

v. Webster-Hayne

w. Texas

x. South Carolina

y. Mexican War

Match these people (each answer, 2 points).

26. _____ Commanded the Texas army, senator from Texas

27. _____ President who added the most land to the U.S.

28. _____ Mexican War hero, president

29. _____ Invented the telegraph

30. _____ Senator, spoke for liberty and union

31. _____ Shortest presidency in history, "Tippecanoe and Tyler, too"

32. _____ Invented the steel plow

33. _____ Wanted territories to choose slavery or not for themselves

34. _____ Mexican dictator

35. _____ Led over 300 slaves to freedom in the North

36. _____ Started *The Liberator* newspaper

37. _____ Chosen to be president by Andrew Jackson, had to deal with the Panic of 1837

38. _____ First president born poor, faced the Nullification Crisis

39. _____ The Great Compromiser

40. _____ Seven Southern states seceded when he was elected president.

a. Henry Clay

b. Abraham Lincoln

c. Zachary Taylor

d. Santa Anna

e. Harriet Tubman

f. Andrew Jackson

g. William Henry Harrison

h. Sam Houston

i. Stephen Douglas

j. James Polk

k. William Garrison

l. Daniel Webster

m. Martin Van Buren

n. Samuel Morse

o. John Deere

Answer *true* or *false* (each answer, 2 points).

41. _____ Kansas was called Bleeding Kansas because of fighting between people who did and did not want the tariff.

42. _____ Davy Crockett and William Travis died at the Battle of Goliad.

43. _____ The Gadsden Purchase was land bought from Mexico for a railroad route across the south.

44. _____ Winfield Scott captured Oklahoma in the Black Hawk War.

45. _____ Oregon was divided between the U.S. and Britain by treaty at 49° latitude, by just extending the border with Canada a little further.

46. _____ The Lincoln-Douglas Debates made Douglas popular all over the United States.

47. _____ The Fugitive Slave Act did not allow captured slaves to testify for themselves, post bail or be tried by a jury.

48. _____ Abraham Lincoln was a well-educated land owner from New York.

49. _____ The states that seceded formed a new nation called the Confederate States of America.

50. _____ The Republican Party did not want slavery in the territories.

HISTORY & GEOGRAPHY 505

Unit 5: A Nation Divided

TEACHER NOTES

MATERIALS NEEDED FOR LIFEPAC	
Required	Suggested
(None)	• map of the United States

ADDITIONAL LEARNING ACTIVITIES

Section 1: The Civil War

1. As a class, read in detail about an important Civil War battle. Draw a diagram or make a model of how it was fought.

2. Discuss these questions in class:

    a. Why did the blockade help the Union?

    b. What was the importance of the Emancipation Proclamation?

    c. Why was the Mississippi River so important to both sides?

    d. Why did more soldiers die of disease than bullets?

    e. Was it wise for Grant to give Lee easy terms of surrender?

3. Read the Gettysburg Address. Discuss why it is considered such a great speech.

4. Build a model of the *Merrimac* or the *Monitor*.

5. Do a one- to two-page report on any of these generals: **Union:** Ulysses S. Grant, William T. Sherman, George McClellan, Philip Sheridan, George Thomas; **Confederate:** Robert E. Lee, Stonewall Jackson, Joseph Johnston, Pierre Beauregard, James Longstreet.

6. Do a class project, including models, pictures and stories, on the life of Abraham Lincoln.

7. Do a presentation for the class on any of these subjects: Medicine in the Civil War, Weapons in the Civil War, the Union Navy, the Government of the Confederacy; Blockade Runners, Black Union Soldiers, the Battle of Gettysburg, the Battle of Chancellorsville, the Siege of Vicksburg, Sherman's March to the Sea, Life in the South under the Blockade, Copperheads (people in the North who opposed the war), the Attack on Fort Sumter or the Battle of Chickamauga.

8. Explore the Internet to discover more about the Civil War by searching "American Civil War."

Section 2: Reconstruction

1. Discuss these questions in class:

    a. Why was Reconstruction so difficult?

    b. How would you have treated the South after the Civil War?

    c. Who was right, Andrew Johnson or the Radical Republicans?

d. What is corruption and how does it harm a country?

e. Why was the Fourteenth Amendment important?

f. Should Andrew Johnson have been impeached?

2. Do a report on the Reconstruction government in one southern state.

3. Do a dramatization of the assassination of Abraham Lincoln.

4. Do a play about the impeachment of Andrew Johnson.

5. Do a class project on the lives of Freedmen after the Civil War.

6. Read a book of historical fiction on life in the Civil War and/or Reconstruction.

Section 3: The Gilded Age

1. Do a report on Alaska.

2. Do a class project on the railroads. Collect pictures, stories, maps and reports.

3. Do a one- to two-page report on any of these men: J.P. Morgan, John D. Rockefeller, Andrew Carnegie, Cornelius Vanderbilt, Leland Stanford, Thomas Edison, Alexander Bell, Jay Gould, George Washington Carver, Booker T. Washington, Rutherford B. Hayes, James Garfield, Chester A. Arthur, Grover Cleveland and Benjamin Harrison.

4. Do a class project, including a bulletin board, on settling the West. Include the Homestead Act, outlaws, Plains Indians, cattle drives, mining and the railroad.

5. Find and read the story of an immigrant who came to America between 1850 and 1900.

6. Discuss these questions in class:

a. Was the tariff good or bad?

b. Why would people settle on the Great Plains?

c. Would you Homestead?

d. Why would a monopoly hurt people who had to buy that product?

e. Was America a "land of opportunity?"

7. Write a story about a cowboy on a cattle drive, a European immigrant coming to America or a Homesteader taking land in the West.

8. Explore the Internet by searching these topics: Wild West, American West, Gilded Age, and Progressive Era.

Administer the LIFEPAC Test.

The test is to be administered in one session. Give no help except with directions.

Evaluate the tests and review areas where the students have done poorly.

Review the pages and activities that stress the concepts tested.

If necessary, administer the Alternate LIFEPAC Test.

ANSWER KEYS

SECTION 1

1.1	Montgomery, Alabama; Richmond, Virginia
1.2	James Buchanan
1.3	Crittenden Compromise
1.4	When Confederate troops fired on Union Fort Sumter in April 1861
1.5	Any order: Texas, Arkansas, Louisiana, Tennessee, Mississippi, Alabama, Florida, Georgia, South Carolina, North Carolina, Virginia
1.6	more men, factories, farms, railroads and a navy
1.7	It had only to survive to win. They were fighting on their land and had better generals.
1.8	Blockade the South, capture the Mississippi River, divide the Confederacy and capture the capital
1.9	Britain needed southern cotton for its textile mills.
1.10	The North supplied Britain with food and the British hated slavery.
1.11	Bull Run; 1861
1.12	Robert E. Lee; Stonewall Jackson
1.13	six
1.14	Ulysses S. Grant; William T. Sherman
1.15	Confederacy
1.16	Any order: *Monitor*, *Merrimac*
1.17	Emancipation Proclamation; Antietam
1.18	George McClellan
1.19	Shiloh
1.20	Vicksburg
1.21	Any order: Donelson, Henry
1.22	David Farragut

1.23	Ambrose Burnside
1.24	Joseph Hooker
1.25	Stonewall Jackson
1.26	draft
1.27	Black men
1.28	disease
1.29	Chickamauga
1.30	George Pickett
1.31	George Meade
1.32	Gettysburg Address
1.33	Appomattox Courthouse
1.34	Abraham Lincoln; Andrew Johnson
1.35	Gettysburg
1.36	Sherman's March to the Sea
1.37	destroyed or stole everything in his path
1.38	Ulysses S. Grant
1.39	The soldiers were free if they surrendered their weapons. They could keep their horses and were given food. Officers could keep their pistols.

SELF TEST 1

1.01 b
1.02 c
1.03 g
1.04 i
1.05 j
1.06 f
1.07 a
1.08 h
1.09 d
1.010 e
1.011 Bull Run
1.012 Atlanta
1.013 Antietam
1.014 Appomattox Courthouse
1.015 Gettysburg
1.016 Petersburg
1.017 Vicksburg
1.018 Chickamauga
1.019 Fort Sumter
1.020 Shiloh
1.021 It was the first between two ironclad ships.
1.022 An announcement by Lincoln that freed the slaves in the South.
1.023 It was an attempt to avoid a split in the Union by protecting slavery south of the Missouri Compromise line.
1.024 Soldiers were free if they surrendered their guns. They could keep their horses and were given food. Officers could keep their pistols.
1.025 They were getting food from the Union and hated slavery.
1.026 N
1.027 B
1.028 N
1.029 N
1.030 N
1.031 S
1.032 B
1.033 N & S, actually some blacks went to war in the Confederate army.
1.034 S
1.035 N

SECTION 2

2.1 John Wilkes Booth; Ford's Theater
2.2 Ten Percent Plan
2.3 Black Codes
2.4 Radical Republicans
2.5 Civil Rights Act
2.6 Fourteenth
2.7 Thirteenth
2.8 Thaddeus Stevens
2.9 false
2.10 false
2.11 false
2.12 true
2.13 true
2.14 false
2.15 false
2.16 true
2.17 true
2.18 true
2.19 false
2.20 true
2.21 false
2.22 There was a great deal of corruption and bribery.
2.23 There were many scandals during his time in office because he trusted men who were dishonest.
2.24 Hayes was allowed to become president and he ended Reconstruction.
2.25 They used violence to frighten Black men and stop them from voting.
2.26 The Republicans and the Democrats had different results for four states.
2.27 Railroad officers hired their own company to build track, overcharging for it; Whiskey manufactures paid bribes to avoid taxes.

SELF TEST 2

2.01	g
2.02	e
2.03	a
2.04	d
2.05	b
2.06	h
2.07	i
2.08	j
2.09	f
2.010	c
2.011	Radical
2.012	Ten Percent
2.013	Black Codes
2.014	Thirteenth
2.015	sharecropper
2.016	Carpetbaggers
2.017	Democratic
2.018	Fort Sumter
2.019	Gettysburg
2.020	Union general
2.021	Scalawags
2.022	Blacks
2.023	Fifteenth
2.024	Any order: *Monitor*, *Merrimac*
2.025	Emancipation Proclamation
2.026	Union (North)
2.027	Freedmen's
2.028	Confederacy (South)
2.029	Appomattox Courthouse
2.030	false
2.031	false
2.032	true
2.033	true
2.034	true
2.035	true
2.036	false
2.037	true
2.038	true
2.039	false

SECTION 3

3.1	Alaska
3.2	Transcontinental Railroad
3.3	cattle drives
3.4	Homestead Act
3.5	Union Pacific
3.6	Central Pacific
3.7	$7.2 million
3.8	sod
3.9	railroad
3.10	gold
3.11	railroad towns
3.12	a gold spike
3.13	Andrew Carnegie
3.14	John D. Rockefeller
3.15	J.P. Morgan
3.16	railroads
3.17	Alexander Bell
3.18	Thomas Edison
3.19	farming
3.20	Bessemer Process
3.21	The people who became wealthy from the new industries and they lived in expensive luxury.
3.22	He set up a lab with assistants to work at creating useful products.
3.23	He worked to give away his fortune.
3.24	They got bigger and were built by large corporations
3.25	Rockefeller made his products cheaper than others, bought out his competitors, bribed officials and forced the railroads to pay him low rates
3.26	false
3.27	true
3.28	true
3.29	false
3.30	false
3.31	true
3.32	true
3.33	true
3.34	false
3.35	true
3.36	false
3.37	true
3.38	false
3.39	true
3.40	true
3.41	true
3.42	false
3.43	true
3.44	false

SELF TEST 3

3.01 e
3.02 f
3.03 j
3.04 i
3.05 h
3.06 d
3.07 b
3.08 c
3.09 g
3.010 a
3.011 Alaska
3.012 Homestead Act
3.013 railroad
3.014 Pendleton Act
3.015 South and east
3.016 Reconstruction
3.017 transcontinental railroad
3.018 Thirteenth
3.019 Emancipation Proclamation
3.020 cowboys
3.021 Cattle were fattened in Texas. Then, they were herded north by cowboys across the open plains to railroad towns to be shipped east.

3.022 People who had become rich from the new industries. They spent a great deal of money to live in luxury.
3.023 It kept the price of European goods high so they could charge more for their American-made goods.
3.024 They controlled all sales of a certain product for the country.
3.025 The tariff raised prices for all the goods they had to buy while the railroad overcharged them to ship crops.
3.026 false
3.027 true
3.028 false
3.029 true
3.030 false
3.031 true
3.032 false
3.033 true
3.034 true
3.035 true

LIFEPAC TEST

1. d
2. s
3. h
4. q
5. j
6. o
7. r
8. a
9. k
10. t
11. p
12. i
13. e
14. b
15. l
16. c
17. n
18. f
19. g
20. m
21. Abraham Lincoln
22. William Sherman
23. Andrew Carnegie
24. Andrew Johnson
25. Robert E. Lee
26. Alexander Bell
27. Thadeus Stevens
28. John D. Rockefeller
29. Ulysses S. Grant
30. John Wilkes Booth
31. He worked at it, setting up a lab with assistants to create useful products.
32. More men, factories, farms, railroads and a navy
33. They used violence to force Blacks to stop voting.
34. Alaska was rich in minerals, fish and wood even though it did not have farms.
35. It was all replaced when the party in power changed and workers had to pay money to the party to keep their jobs.
36. true
37. true
38. false
39. true
40. false
41. true
42. true
43. true
44. true
45. true

ALTERNATE LIFEPAC TEST

1. Abraham Lincoln
2. railroads
3. Alaska
4. Fourteenth
5. Robert E. Lee
6. Appomattox Courthouse
7. trusts (monopolies)
8. Ulysses S. Grant
9. civil service
10. Homestead Act
11. *Merrimac*
12. John D. Rockefeller
13. steel
14. Fort Sumter
15. Emancipation Proclamation
16. Ten Percent
17. railroads
18. Freedmen's
19. transcontinental
20. Radical Republicans
21. false; (James Garfield)
22. false; (textile)
23. true
24. true
25. false; (Ulysses S. Grant)
26. false; (Republican Party)
27. false; (Thirteenth Amendment)
28. true
29. false; (Thomas Edison) *or* (telephone)
30. true
31. b
32. c
33. a
34. c
35. a
36. c
37. b
38. b
39. c
40. b

HISTORY & GEOGRAPHY 505

ALTERNATE LIFEPAC TEST

NAME _____

DATE _____

SCORE _____

Complete these sentences (each answer, 3 points).

1. _____ was president of the U.S. during the Civil War.

2. The _____ were the first large corporations in America.

3. The territory of _____ was purchased from Russia for $7.2 million by Secretary William Seward.

4. The_____ Amendment gave former slaves the rights of citizens.

5. The commander of the Confederate army was _____ .

6. The Confederate army surrendered at _____ .

7. Businesses that controlled all the sales of one product in the country were called _____ .

8. _____ was the victorious Union general, but a very poor president.

9. The Pendleton Act reformed the _____ .

10. Under the _____ , people were able to own 160 acres of land by living on it for five years.

11. The first battle of ironclad ships was between the *Monitor* and the _____ .

12. _____ founded the corporation that controlled almost all oil production in America.

13. The Bessemer Process allowed manufacturers to make _____ cheaply.

14. The Civil War began when the Confederacy fired on _____ .

15. Lincoln announced the _____ to free the slaves in the Confederacy after the Union victory at Antietam.

16. President Andrew Johnson's Reconstruction plan was called the _____ Plan.

17. The Interstate Commerce Act was passed to control the _____ .

18. The _____ Bureau tried to help the newly freed slaves start new lives.

19. The Union Pacific and the Central Pacific came from opposite directions to finish the first _____ railroad in 1869.

20. The _____ were Congressmen who wanted to treat the south harshly during Reconstruction.

Write *true* or *false* on the blank. If the answer is *false*, circle the noun (or noun with its adjective) that is wrong (each answer, 2 points). (If the student answers false correctly, but circles the wrong noun, take off 1 point.)

21. _____ John Wilkes Booth assassinated President James Garfield.

22. _____ Andrew Carnegie made his fortune in the textile business.

23. _____ The long cattle drives made the cowboy famous taking cattle north to the railroad for shipment east.

24. _____ The Battle of Gettysburg was the turning point of the Civil War.

25. _____ President Ulysses S. Grant was the first president impeached.

26. _____ After the Reconstruction, the South voted only for the Republican Party for many years.

27. _____ The Thirteenth Amendment gave freed slaves the right to vote.

28. _____ The tariff hurt farmers.

29. _____ Thomas Edison invented the telephone.

30. _____ After the Civil War, corruption was common in business and government.

Choose the correct letter for each item (each answer, 2 points).

31. _____ Which of the following was *not* a Civil War Amendment to the Constitution?
    a. Fourteenth   b. Twelfth   c. Fifteenth

32. _____ Who was president when the first seven states seceded and formed the Confederacy?
    a. Abraham Lincoln   b. Andrew Johnson   c. James Buchanan

33. _____ The Black Codes in the South made the freed slaves into what?
    a. almost slaves   b. sharecroppers   c. voters

34. _____ The Sherman Anti-Trust Act could have been used against what?
    a. Union Pacific   b. Carpetbaggers   c. Standard Oil

35. _____ Which was an advantage for the Confederacy during the Civil War?
    a. generals   b. number of men   c. industry

36. _____ Which was *not* part of the Union strategy in the Civil War?
    a. blockade
    b. capture the Mississippi River
    c. form an alliance with Britain

37. _____ Which Union general destroyed much of Georgia on his March to the Sea?
    a. George McClellan   b. William T. Sherman   c. Stonewall Jackson

38. _____ Who was the president of the Confederacy?
    a. Thadeus Stevens   b. Jefferson Davis   c. David Farragut

39. _____ Which was not part of the Gilded Age?
    a. lavish spending by high society
    b. larger factories run by corporations
    c. successful reforms of business and government

40. _____ Southern men who worked with the Reconstruction government were called?
    a. Carpetbaggers   b. Scalawags   c. Compromisers

HISTORY & GEOGRAPHY 506

Unit 6: A Changing Nation

TEACHER NOTES

MATERIALS NEEDED FOR LIFEPAC	
Required	Suggested
(None)	• map of the United States

ADDITIONAL LEARNING ACTIVITIES

Section 1: The Progressive Era

1. Do a biography on one of these men: Theodore Roosevelt, William H. Taft, Woodrow Wilson, Robert LaFollete, William Jennings Bryan, Hiram Johnson, Charles Evans Hughes, Samuel Gompers.

2. Explore the Internet by searching these topics: tenement history, Ellis Island immigration, Philippine-American War, Spanish-American War, Panama Canal and Rough Riders. Bookmark your favorite sites, and revisit them to help you complete the Section 1 activities.

3. Read a soldier's account of the Spanish-American War.

4. Research and do an oral report on the history of Cuba, the Philippines, Guam or Puerto Rico. Discuss in class whether American rule or interference helped or hurt the island(s).

5. Build a model of the Panama Canal. Discuss the problems of building it.

6. Discuss in class how you would fix these things that needed reform and why:
    a. Working children
    b. Low wages
    c. Fake medicine
    d. Railroads controlling the government by bribes
    e. Unsafe apartments for the poor
    f. Powerful trusts like Standard Oil
    g. Garbage and horse manure collecting on city streets
    h. Political bosses getting rich by overcharging for things the city must buy (like street cars and wastebaskets)

7. Do a class bulletin board or a short skit on immigration through Ellis Island in New York. (See www.ellisisland.org)

8. Research and write a report on the Philippine-American War (the Philippine fight for independence). Discuss whether or not this war was justified.

9. Build a model, map and/or timeline of the Battle for Santiago during the Spanish-American War.

10. Research the Rough Riders. As a class, make a collection of short biographies of the men in the unit.

Section 2: World War I

1. Discuss these questions in class:

    a. Did the United States have to get into World War I?

    b. Was isolationism a good or bad idea?

    c. Was Germany wrong to use U-boats in a war?

    d. What could have been done to make a better peace?

    e. Why would Germany think Mexico would want war with the U.S.? (Hint: Remember the Mexican War.)

2. Do some research on the men who led the Paris Peace Conference. Perform a play about it.

3. Read a book about World War I or someone who fought in it.

4. Do a two-page report on one of these topics: John Pershing, Airplanes in World War I, Trench Warfare, Kaiser Wilhelm II, Life in America during World War I, the *Lusitania*, German U-boats, the League of Nations, Sergeant Alvin York (an American hero in the war), the Meuse-Argonne Offensive.

5. Explore the Internet by searching these topics: World War I, World War I airplanes and World War I photographs.

Section 3: The Roaring Twenties

1. Explore the Internet by searching these topics: Roaring Twenties, radio history/radio invention, automobile history, flappers, Prohibition, Stock Market Crash of 1929 and Great Depression. Bookmark your favorite sites, and revisit them to help you complete the Section 3 activities.

2. Discuss these questions in class:

    a. Why did people become so wild just after fighting a war?

    b. Why was the automobile so important in America?

    c. Why was the behavior of flappers so shocking?

    d. What does God say in the Bible about credit (borrowing)?

    e. In what ways are the 1920s and the current decade alike? How are these eras different?

    f. Why was Lindberg's flight across the Atlantic Ocean so dangerous?

    g. Why was radio such a big change in America?

3. Do a one-page biography of Warren G. Harding, Calvin Coolidge or Herbert Hoover, Charles Lindbergh, Henry Ford or the Wright Brothers.

4. Collect copies of advertising from the 1890s and the 1920s. Compare the two sets and discuss them in class.

5. Get a video tape of a silent movie and watch it (with your parent's permission).

6. Learn to dance the Charleston. Show the class.

7. Discuss in class how the stock market crashed in 1929. Do you think it could happen again?

8. Do a class project on Prohibition. Collect stories and pictures to display in your room.

Administer the LIFEPAC Test.

The test is to be administered in one session. Give no help except with directions.

Evaluate the tests and review areas where the students have done poorly.

Review the pages and activities that stress the concepts tested.

If necessary, administer the Alternate LIFEPAC Test.

ANSWER KEYS

SECTION 1

1.1	Progressive Era		**1.27**	charge up San Juan Hill
1.2	political bosses		**1.28**	Cuba
1.3	Robert La Follette		**1.29**	Philippines
1.4	Muckrakers		**1.30**	"Remember the *Maine*!"
1.5	Knights of Labor		**1.31**	a
1.6	primary elections		**1.32**	d
1.7	Samuel Gompers		**1.33**	c
1.8	recall election		**1.34**	b
1.9	American Federation of Labor		**1.35**	d
1.10	referendum		**1.36**	d
1.11	false		**1.37**	b
1.12	false		**1.38**	a
1.13	true		**1.39**	b
1.14	true		**1.40**	a
1.15	false		**1.41**	c
1.16	true		**1.42**	a
1.17	true		**1.43**	a
1.18	Yellow Press		**1.44**	d
1.19	Any order: Cuba, Guam, the Philippines, Puerto Rico		**1.45**	b
			1.46	a
1.20	Theodore Roosevelt; William Shafter		**1.47**	a
1.21	colonies		**1.48**	b
1.22	*Maine*		**1.49**	b
1.23	William McKinley		**1.50**	a
1.24	world power		**1.51**	a
1.25	four; 1898			
1.26	George Dewey			

SELF TEST 1

1.01	b
1.02	d
1.03	a
1.04	e
1.05	d
1.06	c
1.07	h
1.08	g
1.09	f
1.010	a
1.011	Progressive
1.012	Yellow Press
1.013	political bosses
1.014	Muckrakers
1.015	Square Deal
1.016	referendum
1.017	union
1.018	recall election
1.019	Panama Canal
1.020	primary election
1.021	Any two: public bids on services, parks, schools, fire dishonest workers, better police and fire protection, fairer taxes, building codes, clean water, hospitals, stopped bosses from choosing candidates
1.022	Any two: firing workers who joined a union; hiring thugs to break up strikes; using the police and the courts to stop the unions
1.023	The battleship *Maine* blew up in Havana harbor
1.024	Any two: Guam, Philippines or Puerto Rico
1.025	They wanted to use his popularity, but keep him out of power
1.026	Any two: Theodore Roosevelt, William H. Taft, Woodrow Wilson
1.027	People were angry about the corruption and cheating in America
1.028	The Spanish-American War
1.029	After the Civil War
1.030	An American army attacked the city and the Spanish fleet was forced to leave the harbor. The American fleet destroyed it.

SECTION 2

2.1	Archduke Ferdinand was assassinated in Sarajevo, Bosnia
2.2	They wanted to defeat France quickly by invading through Belgium and then use all of their army against Russia
2.3	America did not want to get involved in the problems of the rest of the world
2.4	Allied Powers: Britain, France, Russia Central Powers: Germany, Austria-Hungary, Italy
2.5	Dollar Diplomacy
2.6	The two sides set up long trenches across from each other protected by barbed wire, machine guns and artillery
2.7	Men ran across the open No Man's Land toward the enemy trenches
2.8	They had a communist revolution
2.9	A Mexican bandit who raided a town on the U.S. border
2.10	Kaiser Wilhelm II
2.11	having an arms race
2.12	Austria-Hungary and Serbia
2.13	isolationist
2.14	Britain: A friend since relations had been improving for 100 years and an important trading partner France: A friend from the Revolution Germany: A nation that was not free, led by a warlike man who could not be trusted since he violated a treaty by invading Belgium
2.15	U-boats
2.16	A British blockade
2.17	the sinking of the *Lusitania*
2.18	Zimmerman
2.19	April 2, 1917
2.20	unrestricted submarine warfare
2.21	Woodrow Wilson
2.22	U-boats sunk ships and could not rescue passengers; blockades usually just captured cargoes with no loss of life
2.23	American Expeditionary Force
2.24	convoy
2.25	John Pershing
2.26	Meuse-Argonne
2.27	doughboys
2.28	Chateau-Thierry
2.29	Belleau; St. Mihiel
2.30	American army arrived in force
2.31	Herbert Hoover
2.32	100,000
2.33	November 11, 1918
2.34	self-determination
2.35	Treaty of Versailles

2.36	Fourteen Points
2.37	League of Nations
2.38	To make the world safe for democracy; To fight the war to end all wars
2.39	U.S., France, Great Britain, Italy
2.40	Adolf Hitler
2.41	Germany
2.42	isolationism
2.43	The U.S. Senate refused to ratify the Treaty of Versailles.
2.44	It was forced to pay the full cost of the war.
2.45	Saar

SELF TEST 2

2.01	e
2.02	c
2.03	a
2.04	h
2.05	j
2.06	d
2.07	b
2.08	g
2.09	i
2.010	f
2.011	b
2.012	b
2.013	c
2.014	d
2.015	a
2.016	c
2.017	b; c
2.018	d
2.019	b
2.020	Spanish-American War
2.021	American Expeditionary Force
2.022	doughboys
2.023	Germany
2.024	Progressive
2.025	Panama Canal
2.026	the *Maine*
2.027	convoy
2.028	primary
2.029	strike
2.030	true
2.031	false
2.032	true
2.033	true
2.034	false
2.035	false
2.036	true
2.037	false
2.038	true
2.039	true

SECTION 3

3.1	true
3.2	true
3.3	false
3.4	true
3.5	true
3.6	false
3.7	true
3.8	false
3.9	true
3.10	false
3.11	false
3.12	true
3.13	false
3.14	alcohol; 21st
3.15	Orville and Wilbur Wright
3.16	Charles Lindbergh
3.17	1920s
3.18	assembly line
3.19	Prohibition
3.20	Model T
3.21	advertising
3.22	speakeasies
3.23	Jazz
3.24	flappers
3.25	criminal gangs
3.26	illegal; free; fun
3.27	*The Great Train Robbery; The Jazz Singer*
3.28	clear daylight
3.29	the Stock Market Crash of 1929
3.30	farming
3.31	stock
3.32	prices must go up
3.33	credit
3.34	they borrowed the money
3.35	they had to repay their loans

SELF TEST 3

3.01	b
3.02	h
3.03	j
3.04	i
3.05	d
3.06	a
3.07	c
3.08	g
3.09	e
3.010	f
3.011	Stock Market Crash of 1929
3.012	Teapot Dome Scandal
3.013	credit
3.014	Model T®
3.015	radio
3.016	Spanish-American War
3.017	Prohibition
3.018	speakeasies
3.019	the assassination of Archduke Ferdinand
3.020	Germany
3.021	true
3.022	false
3.023	true
3.024	false
3.025	true
3.026	true
3.027	false
3.028	false
3.029	true
3.030	false
3.031	true
3.032	false
3.033	true
3.034	true
3.035	true
3.036	true
3.037	true
3.038	false
3.039	false
3.040	true

LIFEPAC TEST

1. The Progressive Movement
2. the charge up San Juan Hill
3. the Meuse-Argonne Offensive
4. Prohibition
5. Panama Canal
6. the destruction of the Spanish fleet in the Philippines by Dewey
7. William McKinley was president
8. the Spanish-American War
9. unions began seriously organizing in America
10. America annexed the Philippines
11. the explosion of the battleship *Maine* in Havana harbor
12. League of Nations
13. Russia
14. Woodrow Wilson
15. the assassination of Archduke Ferdinand
16. unrestricted submarine warfare
17. Stock Market Crash of 1929
18. Henry Ford
19. Muckrakers
20. Theodore Roosevelt
21. flappers
22. John Pershing
23. Spanish-American War
24. Fourteen Points
25. primary election
26. Charles Lindbergh
27. doughboys
28. Prohibition
29. Central Powers
30. U-boats
31. false
32. false
33. true
34. false
35. true
36. false
37. false
38. false
39. false
40. false

ALTERNATE LIFEPAC TEST

1. h
2. m
3. f
4. k
5. l
6. a
7. b
8. i
9. a
10. b
11. c
12. d
13. n
14. g
15. n
16. j
17. e
18. a
19. b
20. k
21. o
22. p
23. l
24. q
25. m
26. b
27. d
28. a
29. u
30. s
31. c
32. t
33. n
34. f
35. e
36. i
37. g
38. r
39. h
40. j
41. Unlimited submarine warfare; Either: "Make the world safe for democracy" or "Fight the war to end all wars"
42. The U.S. battleship *Maine* blew up in Havana harbor; The war marked the point the U.S. was recognized as a world power.
43. Any order: the Philippines, Guam, Puerto Rico
44. The Stock Market Crash of 1929 which was caused by stock speculation
45. The sale of alcohol was forbidden in the U.S.; It failed because too many people drank anyway and it made criminals rich.

HISTORY & GEOGRAPHY 506

ALTERNATE LIFEPAC TEST

NAME _____

DATE _____

SCORE _____

Choose the correct letter for each item. Some will be used more than once (each answer, 2 points).

1. _____ President during the 1920s, many scandals

2. _____ "The business of America is business."

3. _____ Ruler of Germany, World War I

4. _____ Leader of the AF of L

5. _____ His assassination started World War I

6. _____ President of the U.S., World War I

7. _____ Rough Rider, hero of San Juan Hill

8. _____ Progressive governor of Wisconsin

9. _____ Progressive president, reduced the tariff, Federal Reserve

10. _____ Was made McKinley's vice president to get him out of the way, became the first Progressive president

11. _____ Built and flew the first airplane

12. _____ Flew alone across the Atlantic Ocean

13. _____ Created the assembly line to cut costs

14. _____ Defeated the Spanish fleet in the Philippines

15. _____ Built the first car for the working man, the Model T

16. _____ American general, World War I

17. _____ Progressive president, chosen by Roosevelt to follow him in office

18. _____ His plan for peace was called the Fourteen Points

19. _____ Square Deal for the U.S., Big Stick for Panama

a. Woodrow Wilson

b. Theodore Roosevelt

c. Orville and Wilbur Wright

d. Charles Lindbergh

e. William H. Taft

f. Kaiser Wilhelm II

g. George Dewey

h. Warren G. Harding

i. Robert La Follette

j. John Pershing

k. Samuel Gompers

l. Archduke Ferdinand

m. Calvin Coolidge

n. Henry Ford

Match these items (each answer, 2 points).

20. _____ Popular pastime in the 1920s, especially after it started talking with *The Jazz Singer*

21. _____ Newspapers that printed wild stories without much attention to whether or not they were true

22. _____ Ruled cities before the reforms of the 1890s

23. _____ Illegal bar in the 1920s

24. _____ American soldiers, World War I

25. _____ Zimmerman tried to get this country to go to war with America with German help, World War I

26. _____ Name for the wild time following World War I

27. _____ Germany and Austria-Hungary, World War I

28. _____ American foreign policy, the nation returned to it after the Great War

29. _____ One of the Big Four at the Paris Peace Conference

30. _____ Neutral nation invaded by Germany

31. _____ Name for the reforms of the turn of the century, did not continue after World War I

32. _____ Association of nations after World War I that the U.S. did not join

33. _____ An unfair peace that led into the next war

34. _____ Nation that withdrew from World War I because of a communist revolution

35. _____ Allows voters to force the government to make a law they want

36. _____ Too much of the buying and spending in the 1920s was based on this

37. _____ Nation forced to accept full responsibility for World War I and pay all of its costs

38. _____ The American _?_ was the army sent to France in World War I

39. _____ German submarines

40. _____ Brought drama and comedy with advertising into American homes in the 1920s

a. isolationism

b. Roaring Twenties

c. Progressive

d. Central Powers

e. referendum

f. Russia

g. Germany

h. U-boats

i. credit

j. radio

k. movies

l. speakeasy

m. Mexico

n. Treaty of Versailles

o. Yellow Press

p. political bosses

q. doughboys

r. Expeditionary Force

s. Belgium

t. League of Nations

u. France

Answer these questions (each numbered answer, 4 points).

41. What was the main reason the U.S. got into Word War I, and what was one of America's goals in the war? _____

_____

_____

_____

42. What started the Spanish-American War, and why was it important as part of America's growth in power? _____

_____

_____

_____

43. What three islands (Archipelagos) became U.S. colonies after the Spanish-American War?

_____

_____

44. What event started the Great Depression, and why did that event happen?

_____

_____

45. What was Prohibition, and why didn't it work?_____

_____

_____

HISTORY & GEOGRAPHY 507

Unit 7: Depression and War

TEACHER NOTES

MATERIALS NEEDED FOR LIFEPAC	
Required	Suggested
(None)	• world map

ADDITIONAL LEARNING ACTIVITIES

Section 1: Industrial Revolution in England

1. Interview someone who lived during the Great Depression. Tell their story to the class.

2. Discuss in class how your lives would be different if the U.S. were to have another Great Depression.

3. Write a one-page paper on one of the New Deal agencies.

4. Do a class bulletin board on the Great Depression using pictures, short quotes, songs and your own art work.

5. Discuss these questions:

    a. Why did people blame Herbert Hoover for the Depression?

    b. Why did the war end the Depression?

    c. What would make people accept a dictator as their ruler?

    d. Why was appeasing Hitler such a bad idea?

    e. Why did Americans' attitude change so much after Pearl Harbor?

6. Write a paper or do an oral report on one of these topics: Franklin D. Roosevelt, Herbert Hoover, Winston Churchill, the Dust Bowl, the Nazi Party in Germany, Adolf Hitler, Benito Mussolini, the attack on Pearl Harbor, life in Great Britain when Germany was bombing them or the invasion of Poland.

7. Explore the Internet by searching these topics: dust bowl, Pearl Harbor, Nazi Germany and Adolph Hitler.

Section 2: The War in Europe

1. Do a time line for World War II. Include the important events that put the dictators in power as well as battles.

2. Interview someone who served in the armed forces in World War II. Remember women also served. Tell their story to the class.

3. Do a class project on World War II. Include pictures, stories from older friends and relatives and things from that time.

4. Watch a movie about World War II and discuss it in class.

5. Write a one-page paper about someone who survived the Holocaust.

6. Write a one- to two-page biography of Charles de Gaulle, Dwight D. Eisenhower, George Patton, Bernard Montgomery, George Marshall, Erwin Rommel or Joseph Stalin.

7. Do a presentation to the class on one of these topics: the internment of Japanese-Americans, the Battle of the Atlantic, the Battle of Stalingrad, the invasion of North Africa, the invasion of Italy, D-Day, the Battle of the Bulge or production of war goods in America.

8. Have the class read about the Holocaust from different sources. Then, discuss it in class.

9. Read a fiction book about World War II. Do some research and write a one-page paper about what was really true in the book.

10. Read a nonfiction book about World War II. Do a book report.

11. Explore the Internet by searching these topics: World War II, World War II veterans and the Holocaust. NOTE: Some Holocaust sites contain graphic photographs.

Section 3: The War in the Pacific

1. Read a nonfiction book about the war in the Pacific. Do a book report.

2. As a class, recreate the Battle of Midway using paper models.

3. Do a one-page paper on Douglas MacArthur or Chester Nimitz.

4. Make a map of the war in the Pacific, showing the islands that were taken by the Americans, when they were taken and the casualties.

5. Do a report on the atomic bombs that were used in Japan and their effects on the land and the people.

6. Discuss these questions in class:

   a. Should the atomic bomb have been used on Japan?

   b. What made Island Hopping a good strategy?

   c. Was Doolittle's Raid a good idea?

   d. Why was FDR elected to four terms as president?

   e. Is the United Nations a good idea?

7. Do a report on Japan during the war and right after it.

Administer the LIFEPAC Test.

The test is to be administered in one session. Give no help except with directions.

Evaluate the tests and review areas where the students have done poorly.

Review the pages and activities that stress the concepts tested.

If necessary, administer the Alternate LIFEPAC Test.

ANSWER KEYS

SECTION 1

1.1	Herbert Hoover
1.2	the Bonus Expeditionary Force
1.3	1 out of 4
1.4	They wandered across the country looking for work, sleeping in huts and under newspapers, standing in line for food when they couldn't find work
1.5	the dust bowl
1.6	business
1.7	they failed (went out of business)
1.8	The army drove out the people and burned the camp.
1.9	Franklin Delano Roosevelt
1.10	New Deal
1.11	A community of shacks built of tin, cardboard, and wood during the Herbert Hoover era
1.12	A covering of newspapers
1.13	use it to help people or businesses
1.14	the Great Depression/New Deal
1.15	Good Neighbor Policy
1.16	Relief, Recovery and Reform
1.17	Civilian Conservation Corp
1.18	Securities and Exchange Commission
1.19	Hundred Days
1.20	deficit spending
1.21	a Bank Holiday
1.22	Work Progress Administration

1.23	Tennessee Valley Authority
1.24	Federal Emergency Relief Administration
1.25	National Labor Relations Board
1.26	Supreme Court
1.27	World War II
1.28	Benito Mussolini; Adolf Hitler; Joseph Stalin
1.29	Winston Churchill
1.30	swastika
1.31	*blitzkrieg*
1.32	Poland
1.33	Vichy France
1.34	Dunkirk
1.35	Czechoslovakia
1.36	master; Jewish
1.37	Manchuria; Ethiopia
1.38	Great Britain
1.39	Berlin-Rome-Tokyo Axis
1.40	the Soviet Union
1.41	FDR
1.42	Lend-Lease
1.43	Atlantic Charter
1.44	*Arizona*
1.45	December 7, 1941
1.46	oil and metal
1.47	aircraft carriers
1.48	the Japanese attack on Pearl Harbor
1.49	over 2,000

SELF TEST 1

1.01	c
1.02	e
1.03	f
1.04	d
1.05	c
1.06	d
1.07	d
1.08	a
1.09	b
1.010	a
1.011	New Deal
1.012	Bank Holiday
1.013	World War II
1.014	Bonus Army
1.015	Good Neighbor Policy
1.016	Tennessee Valley Authority
1.017	Lend-Lease
1.018	dust bowl
1.019	Hundred Days
1.020	Civilian Conservation Corp
1.021	Germany invaded Poland
1.022	1 out of 4
1.023	League of Nations
1.024	swastika
1.025	Great Britain
1.026	Berlin-Rome-Tokyo Axis
1.027	Soviet Union
1.028	the Japanese attack on Pearl Harbor
1.029	Atlantic Charter
1.030	Czechoslovakia
1.031	true
1.032	true
1.033	false
1.034	true
1.035	false
1.036	false
1.037	false
1.038	true
1.039	true
1.040	false

SECTION 2

2.1	15 million
2.2	the home front
2.3	It provided the arms, food, ships, and supplies the Allies needed to win the war.
2.4	Battle of the Atlantic
2.5	Victory Garden
2.6	wolf packs
2.7	Pearl Harbor and the Aleutian Islands in Alaska
2.8	They used warships and planes to attack subs, convoys to move ships and sonar to find the enemy subs
2.9	They were united and willing to do whatever was needed to win the war.
2.10	They were forced to move into internment camps away from the coast.
2.11	North Africa; Italy
2.12	Stalingrad (Volgograd)
2.13	Dwight D. Eisenhower
2.14	Any order: Bernard Montgomery, George Patton
2.15	Bernard Montgomery, El Alamein
2.16	Charles de Gaulle
2.17	Erwin Rommel
2.18	the Soviet Union; winter
2.19	Sicily
2.20	Germans
2.21	Vichy France
2.22	a month
2.23	Joseph Stalin
2.24	May; 1945
2.25	D-Day
2.26	Any order: Omaha, Utah
2.27	Overlord
2.28	Holocaust
2.29	V-E Day
2.30	Calais
2.31	August 1944
2.32	George Patton
2.33	June 6, 1944
2.34	committed suicide
2.35	Nuremberg, Germany
2.36	Soviet
2.37	Omaha
2.38	Battle of the Bulge
2.39	6 million

SELF TEST 2

2.01	i
2.02	j
2.03	f
2.04	c
2.05	a
2.06	h
2.07	e
2.08	b
2.09	g
2.010	d
2.011	Normandy
2.012	New Deal
2.013	Vichy France
2.014	Pearl Harbor
2.015	Holocaust
2.016	Hundred Days
2.017	World War II
2.018	Germany invaded Poland
2.019	Battle of the Atlantic
2.020	(Berlin-Rome-Tokyo) Axis
2.021	d
2.022	b
2.023	b
2.024	a
2.025	c
2.026	b
2.027	d
2.028	b
2.029	d
2.030	b
2.031	false
2.032	false
2.033	true
2.034	true
2.035	true
2.036	false
2.037	true
2.038	true
2.039	false
2.040	false

SECTION 3

3.1	Midway
3.2	did not see each other
3.3	Doolittle's Raid
3.4	*Lexington; Yorktown*
3.5	Bataan; Corregidor
3.6	airplanes
3.7	Bataan Death March
3.8	Burma Road
3.9	Douglas MacArthur
3.10	four
3.11	broken the Japanese code
3.12	Port Moresby; New Guinea
3.13	Island Hopping or leapfrogging
3.14	Douglas MacArthur
3.15	hop over
3.16	surrender
3.17	Guadalcanal
3.18	Gilbert; Marshall; Marianas
3.19	the Philippine Sea
3.20	Leyte Gulf
3.21	7,000
3.22	Okinawa
3.23	Japan
3.24	false
3.25	true
3.26	false
3.27	false
3.28	true
3.29	false
3.30	false
3.31	true
3.32	true
3.33	false
3.34	false
3.35	true
3.36	false
3.37	true
3.38	false
3.39	false

SELF TEST 3

3.01 To hop over fortified islands, capture less fortified ones to use as bases to attack the next islands

3.02 The program to build an American atomic bomb

3.03 They retreated to the Bataan Peninsula and Corregidor Island, surrendered when they grew weak from lack of food, were forced to march to prison camps and were killed if they collapsed

3.04 The first navy battle in which the ships did not see each other

3.05 to the death

3.06 The Japanese attacked Pearl Harbor, Hawaii, without warning on December 7, 1941

3.07 The invasion of Normandy, France

3.08 An organization of nations, created at the end of World War II.

3.09 American bombers took off from aircraft carriers, bombed Tokyo and crash-landed in China.

3.010 President Truman used it to avoid the deaths that would have occurred if the Allies had invaded Japan.

3.011 false; change Charles de Gaulle to Benito Mussolini

3.012 false; change Great Britain to Germany

3.013 true

3.014 false; change Franklin D. Roosevelt to Harry S. Truman

3.015 true

3.016 true

3.017 false; change Soviet Union to Germany

3.018 true

3.019 true

3.020 false; change Franklin Roosevelt to Herbert Hoover

3.021 false; change France to Poland

3.022 false; change El Alamein to Stalingrad

3.023 false; change The New Deal to World War II

3.024 false; change Central Powers to Axis Powers

3.025 true

3.026 true

3.027 false; change German to American

3.028 false; change Utah to Omaha

3.029 true

3.030 true

LIFEPAC TEST

1. c
2. d
3. h
4. i
5. g
6. a
7. j
8. b
9. e
10. f
11. Island Hopping
12. Poland
13. atomic bombs
14. Japan; Pearl Harbor
15. World War II
16. 1; 4
17. Midway
18. Soviet Union
19. Normandy, France
20. Manhattan
21. Coral
22. Holocaust
23. Stalingrad
24. North Africa
25. Doolittle's
26. Civilian Conservation Corp
27. Lend-Lease
28. Italy
29. United Nations
30. League; Nations
31. true
32. false
33. false
34. true
35. true
36. false
37. false
38. true
39. true
40. false

ALTERNATE LIFEPAC TEST

1. c
2. q
3. p
4. e
5. a
6. s
7. n
8. k
9. j
10. o
11. m
12. g
13. f
14. b
15. h
16. l
17. i
18. d
19. r
20. t
21. Hiroshima or Nagasaki
22. a bank holiday
23. four
24. Dwight D. Eisenhower
25. Winston Churchill
26. United Nations
27. to the death
28. Vichy France
29. Bataan Death March
30. the Holocaust
31. true
32. true
33. false; change Germany to Japan
34. false; change The Soviet Union to Italy
35. false; change Joseph Stalin to Adolf Hitler
36. false; change three to four
37. true
38. false; change Benito Mussolini to Adolf Hitler
39. true
40. false; change British army to Free French

HISTORY & GEOGRAPHY 507

ALTERNATE LIFEPAC TEST

NAME _____

DATE _____

SCORE _____

Match these items (each item, 2 points).

1. _____ Turning point of the Pacific war

2. _____ FDR's policy toward the other American nations

3. _____ American strategy in the Pacific war

4. _____ Japanese attack on the U.S. navy in Hawaii, got the U.S. into the war

5. _____ The reaction of most Americans when the war began

6. _____ Invading the Soviet Union without preparing for winter warfare

7. _____ American bombing attack on Tokyo launched from aircraft carriers, planes crashed in China

8. _____ Place where the Allies invaded France, June 6, 1944

9. _____ The first Allied invasion in the war in Europe after America joined the war, Operation Torch

10. _____ U.S. plan to supply the Allies with what they needed to win the war

11. _____ World War II started when Germany invaded

12. _____ Battle between German submarines and the Allies trying to get supplies to Europe

13. _____ Event that ended the Great Depression

14. _____ American program to build an atomic bomb

15. _____ First navy battle in which the ships did not see each other

16. _____ Location of the worst fighting on D-Day

17. _____ First British victory of the war, Egypt

18. _____ Turning point of the war in Europe

19. _____ FDR's program to end the Great Depression

20. _____ The early part of FDR's presidency when many laws were passed quickly

a. isolationism

b. Manhattan Project

c. Midway

d. Stalingrad

e. Pearl Harbor

f. World War II

g. Atlantic

h. Coral Sea

i. El Alamein

j. North Africa

k. Normandy

l. Omaha

m. Poland

n. Doolittle's Raid

o. Lend-Lease

p. Island Hopping

q. Good Neighbor

r. New Deal

s. Hitler's big mistake

t. Hundred Days

Give the information requested (each answer, 3 points).

21. Name one of the cities hit by an atomic bomb at the end of World War II.
_____

22. FDR's first action after becoming president _____

23. The number of times FDR was elected president _____

24. Supreme Allied commander for the invasions in Europe _____
_____

25. Prime Minister of Great Britain, World War II _____

26. Organization of nations after World War II _____

27. How Japanese soldiers fought on the Pacific islands _____

28. Part of France not occupied by Germany _____

29. U.S. prisoners were forced to walk to prison camps in the Philippines and were killed if they
collapsed _____

30. Millions of innocent people killed in Nazi Germany, especially Jews
_____

Write *true* or *false* in the blank. If the answer is *false*, change one or more of the underlined words to make it true (each numbered answer, 3 points). (If a student correctly answers false, but cannot make the correct change, take off 1 point.)

31. _____ Herbert Hoover was the president blamed for the Great Depression.

32. _____ Harry S. Truman was president at the end of World War II.

33. _____ Douglas MacArthur was the military governor of Germany after the war

34. _____ The Soviet Union tried to surrender when the Allies invaded Sicily, but Germany would not allow it.

35. _____ Joseph Stalin committed suicide when his nation was defeated at the end of World War II.

36. _____ At the worst part of the Great Depression, one out of three people were out of work.

37. _____ Before the Great Depression the American government had never used its money to feed people, help businesses or create jobs.

38. _____ Benito Mussolini hated Jews and believed his people were a master race.

39. _____ In America, food and other goods were rationed during the war.

40. _____ Charles de Gaulle was the leader of the British Army.

HISTORY & GEOGRAPHY 508

Unit 8: Cold War

TEACHER NOTES

MATERIALS NEEDED FOR LIFEPAC	
Required	Suggested
(None)	• world map

ADDITIONAL LEARNING ACTIVITIES

Section 1: Communist Threat

1. All students should do a report on or be part of a class discussion about communism. Teachers should help them understand why it looked so good in theory, but was so awful in fact. (See the Teacher's Reference on Communism at the end of this section.).

2. Do a class project on the Communist Bloc. Have each student choose a communist country, research it and report to the class about how communism took control there and what happened because of it. Then, discuss what they learned as a class.

3. Do a paper on atomic bombs and the Cold War. What kinds were made, how many and where were they kept?

4. Do a report or paper on the space race. This topic can be divided into many parts for the United States: the Mercury Program, the Gemini Program, the Apollo Program, Skylab, space probes, satellites, International Space Station, and the Space Shuttle.

5. Do a report about Berlin during the Cold War.

6. Collect pictures for a bulletin board about what the cities of Europe looked like just after World War II. Discuss why the Marshall Plan was so important for these people.

7. Do a report on one of these topics: the Hungarian Revolution of 1956, the Czechoslovakia Uprising or Prague Spring of 1968, NATO, the Berlin Airlift, Taiwan, Chiang Kai-shek, Mao Zedong, George Marshall or Joseph McCarthy.

8. Discuss these questions:

    a. Why wouldn't you like to live in a communist country?

    b. Should the U.S. have tried to stop communism?

    c. Was Taiwan the real government of China?

    d. Why were people so quick to believe Joseph McCarthy?

    e. How would you describe the Cold War?

9. Write and perform a short play on the Berlin Airlift.

10. Explore the Internet by searching these topics: cold war, space race and NASA.

11. An advanced project would be for a student to research the websites of the Communist Party of China. Then, discuss with an adult how some of the articles distort the truth and why. This could be a class project.

Communism (Teacher's Reference)

Communism is based on the ideas of Karl Marx and Friedrich Engels. Together they wrote a pamphlet in 1848 called the *Communist Manifesto*. It was written when the Industrial Revolution was causing a great deal of suffering in Europe. Eventually, the reform movements in Western Europe and America would correct the long hours, poor pay and dangerous working conditions of the laboring class, called the *proletariat*. They would become prosperous members of the middle class in the 20th Century.

However, Marx and Engels saw the evils of capitalism and did not foresee the reforms. Instead, they predicted that capitalism would always exploit the proletariat. The injustices would cause a huge class war between the proletariat and the *bourgeoisie* (the ruling class/business owners). Marx believed the proletariat would win this violent struggle. They would set up a *dictatorship of the proletariat* which would take all the means of production (land and factories). The dictatorship would eliminate all classes and, thus, all conflict in the nation. With common ownership of everything and no classes to fight with each other, perfect peace and happiness would result. This was communism, a state in which all institutions, like governments, churches, and armies, would fade away because no one would need them. Everyone would work for the common good and get all they needed to survive. It would be utopia.

Obviously, the most fundamental flaw in the communist theory occurs because man is not capable of making a perfect society because he is a sinful, imperfect being. However, it is this idealism, this dream of utopia that attracted so many oppressed people and liberal intellectuals to communism. In countries like Russia in early 1900s, where political power and wealth were held by a very few people, it was a very seductive idea. It completely failed when Lenin tried to put it into practice in Russia after the Communist Revolution there in 1917.

What Lenin tried to do was create a dictatorship of the proletariat using a small number of people who claimed to *represent* the proletariat. These people were, of course, Lenin and his chosen followers, the Communist Party. The party, as the representative of the proletariat, took control of the government, eliminated all classes, took over ownership of all the means of production and eliminated all capitalist influences (people who disagreed with communism). Then, in this perfect, classless society, the state and its institutions were supposed to fade away into perfect communism. That was Lenin's theory, at least.

What happened in fact could easily have been predicted. The "representatives of the proletariat" were more interested in increasing and maintaining their own power than creating a perfect society. They set up privileges for themselves, killed or imprisoned opponents, and made free use of secret police and lawless methods, all in the name of the oppressed people. The leaders claimed that this system produced happier people, better products and a freer society than capitalism. It was this lie that was the basis for the whole system. If communism was not a better system, the communist rulers could not justify their dictatorship. They continued to pretend they were attempting to create a state of utopia. They claimed they were close to it and that their people were much better off than the "oppressed workers" under capitalism.

The power of the Soviet Union forced the system on eastern Europe. Oppressed people in the Third World believed the lies and tried to create this utopia in their lands for years. However, the wealth and stability of the capitalist nations made the lie look sillier and sillier as the 20th Century continued. Finally, the lack of technological advances and the general poverty of communist nations forced the truth out into the open when Mikhail Gorbachev tried his reforms in the U.S.S.R. The house of cards collapsed under the hand of truth in 1989.

Section 2: Hot War and Crises

1. Have someone who was in the Korean War or Vietnam War speak to your class. Think about questions to ask ahead of time.

2. Research and do a paper or report on the United Nations.

3. Make three large maps of Korea. Show the furthest North Korean advance and the landing at Inchon on one. Show the furthest U.N. advance on the second. Show Korea today on the third.

4. Read a nonfiction book about the Korean or Vietnam War. Do a book report.

5. Do a report on one of these people: Douglas MacArthur, Ho Chi Minh, Nikita Khrushchev or Fidel Castro.

6. Do a bulletin board on the Korean War or Vietnam War, include a map.

7. Discuss these questions:

    a. Was it wrong for the U.S. to spy on the Soviet Union?

    b. What could have gone wrong in the Cuban Missile Crisis?

    c. Was how we got out of Vietnam a good way or not?

    d. What was wrong with the Gulf of Tonkin Resolution? (Hint: Congress is supposed to declare war.)

8. Write a two-page paper on the history of Cuba, Vietnam or Korea.

9. Explore the Internet by searching these topics: Korean War and Vietnam War.

Section 3: Upheaval in America

1. Do a class project on "separate but equal." Find out what African-American facilities were like in the South before 1950. Discuss in class.

2. Do a bulletin board on the Civil Rights movement.

3. Write a one-page paper on what it would be like for you to be the first African-American person to attend a school that had always been for whites only.

4. Do a report on one of these people: Martin Luther King, John Kennedy, Lyndon Johnson, Robert Kennedy or Earl Warren.

5. Interview people who were between 15 and 25 in the 1960s and ask them what they thought of the protests and ideas. Then, interview people who were over 30 in the 1960s, ask the same questions. Discuss what you learned in class.
    (This can be an individual or class project.)

6. Have a 60s day at school. Dress in 60s clothes. Bring in pictures and art from that time period to decorate the room.

7. Teachers: Discuss rebellion in the 1960s as bad seed and the fruit we harvest today from it.

8. Ask someone who is old enough to remember what they were doing when they learned that John Kennedy had been shot. Ask them how his death affected them. Discuss the answers you got in class.

9. Explore the Internet by searching these topics: Civil Rights movement and Martin Luther King, Jr.

ANSWER KEYS

SECTION 1

1.1 Any order: Poland, East Germany, Romania, Bulgaria, Hungary, Soviet Union, Czechoslovakia, Albania, Yugoslavia

1.2 no

1.3 It was kept separate from the western parts and made into a communist nation.

1.4 That they would fight a nuclear war and destroy all life on Earth

1.5 United States, Great Britain, France and the Soviet Union

1.6 U.S.S.R. and the United States

1.7 the Western World or Free World

1.8 Eastern Bloc or Communist Bloc

1.9 Non-aligned or Third World

1.10 everything; freedom; lies

1.11 Iron Curtain

1.12 equality

1.13 Berlin Airlift

1.14 containment

1.15 Marshall Plan

1.16 Berlin Wall

1.17 George Marshall

1.18 Harry S. Truman

1.19 Any order: Czechoslovakia, Hungary

1.20 Solidarity

1.21 NATO

1.22 Warsaw Pact

1.23 One group tried to spread communism in a country with Soviet help, while another tried to stop them with American help.

1.24 the U.S.S.R. would not allow it

1.25 Turkey and Greece

1.26 the skilled, smart, capable people

1.27 North Atlantic Treaty Organization

1.28 Chiang Kai-shek

1.29 Mao Zedong; Chiang Kai-shek

1.30 Great Leap Forward

1.31 Taiwan

1.32 Cultural Revolution

1.33 enemies

1.34 An unfair, large hunt for wrongdoing based on fear

1.35 People had money saved up during the war to spend on all kinds of manufactured goods.

1.36 Fair Deal

1.37 "I like Ike"

1.38 A State Department worker who lied about being a communist spy

1.39 A couple executed for giving American atomic bomb secrets to the Soviets

1.40 By accusing people of being communists without proof when everyone was afraid of communists

1.41 Hearings on TV

1.42 NASA

1.43 Sputnik, Soviet Union

1.44 United States, 1969

1.45 the Soviet Union in 1961

1.46 He was censured.

SELF TEST 1

1.01	g
1.02	f
1.03	h
1.04	i
1.05	d
1.06	e
1.07	a
1.08	c
1.09	b
1.010	A government that owns everything, allows no freedom and lies to control its people
1.011	They were forced to become and remain communist by the U.S.S.R.
1.012	The U.S. would help any nation to stop communism from spreading to their land.
1.013	The U.S. led the Free World or Western World; the Soviet Union led the Communist Bloc or Eastern Bloc
1.014	People had saved money during the war and now wanted to spend it on things.
1.015	Americans saw eastern Europe and China lose their freedom and did not want it to happen to them.
1.016	People are not paid more for better work and are not fired for bad work.
1.017	They were afraid a nuclear war might destroy all life on Earth.
1.018	The nation and capital were divided into four parts occupied by the U.S., France, Britain and the U.S.S.R.
1.019	To make China into an industrial power in just a few years.
1.020	Berlin Wall
1.021	Taiwan
1.022	Marshall Plan
1.023	Berlin Airlift
1.024	Solidarity
1.025	NATO
1.026	Sputnik
1.027	NASA
1.028	Iron Curtain
1.029	Warsaw Pact
1.030	false
1.031	true
1.032	true
1.033	false
1.034	false
1.035	false

SECTION 2

2.1	Douglas MacArthur
2.2	North Korea invaded South Korea
2.3	communist
2.4	Taiwan held the Chinese seat at the United Nations
2.5	Pusan Perimeter
2.6	Inchon
2.7	return home
2.8	fired him
2.9	38th parallel
2.10	the Chinese army
2.11	the United Nations
2.12	1953
2.13	Nikita Khrushchev
2.14	thaw
2.15	U-2
2.16	The U.S. backed one side and the U.S.S.R. the other.
2.17	a. The U.S. learned that the U.S.S.R. was building missile bases in Cuba. b. He had the navy blockade the island to stop delivery of the missiles. c. The Soviets agreed not to deliver the missiles and took down the bases.
2.18	Fidel Castro
2.19	Francis Gary Powers
2.20	Bay of Pigs
2.21	A war to force a nation to become communist
2 22	The Soviets left and it became a united, free country
2.23	false
2.24	false
2.25	true
2.26	false
2.27	false
2.28	false
2.29	true
2.30	false
2.31	true
2.32	true
2.33	true
2.34	true
2.35	false

SELF TEST 2

2.01	b
2.02	f
2.03	i
2.04	d
2.05	j
2.06	e
2.07	h
2.08	g
2.09	a
2.010	c
2.011	North Korea
2.012	Pusan Perimeter
2.013	containment
2.014	Bay of Pigs
2.015	Communist
2.016	Marshall Plan
2.017	NATO
2.018	North
2.019	all
2.020	China

2.021 MacArthur wanted to attack China. Truman ordered him not to do it. The general tried to publicly fight the orders.

2.022 They insisted that their prisoners, held by the U.N., had to be forced to return home.

2.023 A time when the two sides were nicer and tried to work out problems

2.024 The U.S.S.R. tried to put missiles in Cuba. The U.S. blockaded the island until the Soviets agreed not to send the missiles and took down the bases.

2.025 The U.S. helped one side while the U.S.S.R. helped the other.

2.026 A resolution by Congress that gave the president power to do whatever was needed to stop the Vietnamese communists.

2.027 The communists just kept fighting, getting more men and supplies from North Vietnam which was resupplied by China and the U.S.S.R.

2.028 A wall around West Berlin was built to keep East Germans from fleeing to freedom through the city.

2.029 The dividing line between free and communist Europe.

2.030 The Soviet Union invaded and put communism back in power.

2.031	true
2.032	true
2.033	true
2.034	false
2.035	true

SECTION 3

3.1 Martin Luther King, Jr.

3.2 peaceful

3.3 Montgomery Bus Boycott

3.4 "I Have a Dream;" Washington

3.5 Jim Crow

3.6 Civil Rights; Voting Rights

3.7 *Plessy v. Ferguson; Brown v. Board of Education of Topeka*

3.8 soldiers

3.9 Rosa Parks

3.10 1968

3.11 the Vietnam War

3.12 Any order: Dwight Eisenhower, John Kennedy, Lyndon Johnson, Richard Nixon

3.13 The large group of people born in the years right after World War II

3.14 More divorce, abortion and drug use

3.15 They refused to register for it or fled the country when they were drafted.

3.16 Earl Warren

3.17 Lee Harvey Oswald; James Earl Ray

3.18 Young people who rebelled against everything

3.19 Anti-war protesters fought with the police and it was shown on TV.

3.20 He was able to get a ceasefire in 1973 and pulled the soldiers out during it.

3.21 Great Society, the Vietnam War cost too much

3.22 New Frontier; it was passed under Johnson after Kennedy was assassinated.

3.23 A program to let Americans help people in poorer countries, started by Kennedy

3.24 Lyndon Johnson

3.25 (Answers will vary). It was the longest, most controversial war in our history and the first in which we failed.

SELF TEST 3

3.01 f
3.02 i
3.03 a
3.04 d
3.05 j
3.06 g
3.07 e
3.08 h
3.09 c
3.010 b
3.011 Jim Crow
3.012 Vietnam War
3.013 Baby Boomers
3.014 Cuban Missile Crisis
3.015 Iron Curtain
3.016 NATO
3.017 Mao Zedong
3.018 "I Have a Dream"
3.019 Sputnik
3.020 Taiwan

3.021 African Americans had separate schools and facilities that were not as good as those set aside for white people.
3.022 They were taken to school and protected by soldiers.
3.023 They peacefully protested and refused to obey the laws.
3.024 More divorce, abortion and drug use
3.025 They refused to register or fled the country when they were drafted.
3.026 It was the longest, most controversial war in American history and we failed to win.
3.027 A government that owns everything, allows no freedom and lies to control its people
3.028 It gained equal legal rights for African Americans.
3.029 A wall built around West Berlin to keep East Germans from escaping to freedom through the city
3.030 The U.S. would help any nation to keep communism from spreading to their land.
3.031 false
3.032 true
3.033 true
3.034 false
3.035 false

LIFEPAC TEST

1. Communism
2. Douglas MacArthur
3. Berlin Wall
4. Gulf of Tonkin
5. Nationalist or Taiwan
6. Cuba
7. Marshall Plan
8. Iron Curtain
9. communists
10. NASA
11. c
12. c
13. a
14. b
15. d
16. b
17. a
18. d
19. d
20. b
21. true
22. false; change <u>Soviet</u> to <u>U.S.</u>
23. false; change <u>France</u> to <u>Germany</u>
24. false; change <u>Confrontation</u> to <u>Containment</u>
25. false; change <u>Germans</u> to <u>Soviets</u>
26. true
27. true
28. false; change <u>Lyndon Johnson</u> to <u>John or Robert Kennedy</u>
29. false; change <u>The Warsaw Pact</u> to <u>NATO</u>
30. false; change <u>East Germany</u> to the <u>Soviet Union</u>

ALTERNATE LIFEPAC TEST

1. g
2. l
3. e
4. n
5. p
6. q
7. c
8. r
9. j
10. a
11. i
12. f
13. b
14. o
15. h
16. m
17. k
18. d
19. f
20. q
21. g
22. o
23. k
24. s
25. i
26. t
27. r
28. v
29. b
30. c
31. d
32. p
33. u
34. a
35. m
36. l
37. e
38. h
39. j
40. n
41. true
42. false
43. true
44. true
45. false
46. false
47. true
48. false
49. true
50. true

HISTORY & GEOGRAPHY 508

ALTERNATE LIFEPAC TEST

NAME _____

DATE _____

SCORE _____

Match these people (each item, 2 points).

1. _____ Korean War commander, saved Korea by landing at Inchon

2. _____ Nationalist leader in China, fled to Taiwan

3. _____ Communist leader in Vietnam

4. _____ Supreme Court Justice, supported Civil Rights, banned prayer in schools

5. _____ President, Great Society, sent soldiers to Vietnam to fight

6. _____ Communist Chinese leader, won the civil war

7. _____ State Department worker who lied about being a communist spy

8. _____ U-2 spy plane pilot, shot down over the U.S.S.R.

9. _____ President who started containment and fired the Korean commander for publically fighting orders

10. _____ Young president, New Frontier, assassinated

11. _____ Civil Rights leader, assassinated in 1968

12. _____ Communist leader of Cuba

13. _____ Senator who made wild accusations about communists in the government

14. _____ Ended U.S. fighting in Vietnam

15. _____ President, popular war hero, began the U.S. highway system

16. _____ African-American woman who began the Civil Rights movement when she refused to move to the back of the bus

17. _____ U.S. general in World War II, Secretary of State after the war

18. _____ Soviet leader who wanted peaceful coexistence with the free nations

a. John Kennedy

b. Joseph McCarthy

c. Alger Hiss

d. Nikita Khrushchev

e. Ho Chi Minh

f. Fidel Castro

g. Douglas MacArthur

h. Dwight Eisenhower

i. Martin Luther King

j. Harry S. Truman

k. George Marshall

l. Chiang Kai-shek

m. Rosa Parks

n. Earl Warren

o. Richard Nixon

p. Lyndon Johnson

q. Mao Zedong

r. Francis Powers

Match these items (each answer, 2 points).

19. _____ Built to keep East Germans from escaping communism

20. _____ Peace talks were stopped because the communists wanted prisoners to be forced to go home

21. _____ U.S. joined other nations to protect Europe from the Soviet Union during the Cold War

22. _____ Supreme Court's words that allowed segregation of Blacks in 1896, *Plessy v. Ferguson*

23. _____ Widespread protests against this in the 1960s and 1970s

24. _____ Soviet Union tried to put missiles near the U.S., Kennedy stopped them with a blockade

25. _____ American space agency

26. _____ Large group of people born right after World War II

27. _____ Fought the communists in Korea

28. _____ Successful attempt to get equal legal rights for Blacks

29. _____ Dividing line between communist and free in Europe

30. _____ Government set up in nations conquered by the U.S.S.R.

31. _____ Fear of this prevented a super power war

32. _____ Event that started the Civil Rights movement

33. _____ Allows Americans to help people in poorer countries

34. _____ U.S. gave money to rebuild Europe after World War II

35. _____ U.S.-trained Cubans failed to retake communist Cuba

36. _____ First man-made satellite

37. _____ U.S. policy to keep communism from spreading

38. _____ Communist treaty organization in east Europe

39. _____ Soviets blockaded the German capital to force the western powers to leave, they did this instead

40. _____ Resolution allowing the president to do whatever was needed to stop the Vietnamese communists

a. Marshall Plan

b. Iron Curtain

c. communist

d. nuclear war

e. containment

f. Berlin Wall

g. NATO

h. Warsaw Pact

i. NASA

j. Berlin Airlift

k. Vietnam War

l. Sputnik

m. Bay of Pigs

n. Gulf of Tonkin

o. separate but equal

p. Montgomery Bus Boycott

q. Korean War

r. United Nations

s. Cuban Missile Crisis

t. Baby Boomers

u. Peace Corp

v. Civil Rights movement

Answer *true* or *false* (each answer, 2 points).

41. _____ The rebellions of the 1960s led to more divorce, abortion and drug use today.

42. _____ Communism is a kind of government that thinks truth and honesty is important.

43. _____ China claimed that its soldiers who fought in the Korean War were volunteers.

44. _____ All over the world during the Cold War the U.S. would take one side in a war and the Soviet Union would take the other.

45. _____ Americans had no fears about communism in the 1950s.

46. _____ Germany was divided into two parts at the end of World War II with the U.S. occupying half and the Soviet Union the other half.

47. _____ Communist countries are often called republics or democracies.

48. _____ Desegregation went smoothly and easily, without violence in the South.

49. _____ The U.S. did not win the Vietnam War and many people had different reasons for why that happened.

50. _____ Many of John Kennedy's ideas were passed by Congress after he died.

HISTORY & GEOGRAPHY 509

Unit 9: America into the New Millennium

TEACHER NOTES

MATERIALS NEEDED FOR LIFEPAC	
Required	Suggested
(None)	• world map

ADDITIONAL LEARNING ACTIVITIES

Section 1: Fall of a President

1. Write a paper or give a report in class about Richard Nixon, Gerald Ford, Jimmy Carter, Henry Kissinger, Anwar Sadat or Menachem Begin.

2. Make a time line of the Watergate Scandal. Discuss in class what Nixon did that was wrong.

3. Research Nixon's trip to China or the Soviet Union. Pretend to be a reporter and give a newscast about these historic events.

4. Discuss theses questions:

    a. Why was the Iran Hostage Crisis so frustrating for America?

    b. Could we have another energy crisis?

    c. Why was it easier for Begin and Sadat to negotiate in America?

    d. What kind of problems does inflation cause?

    e. Would you have pardoned Richard Nixon?

    f. Why was it so bad that the hostages in Iran came from the embassy?

5. Hold a mock impeachment trial of Richard Nixon and decide whether or not to remove him from office.

6. Read old magazine articles on the Iran Hostage Crisis.

7. Do a one- to two-page report on the Soviet invasion of Afghanistan. What happened? How did the U.S. respond? Why couldn't they win?

8. Explore the Internet by searching "Watergate scandal" to discover more about this event.

Section 2: Rebuilding Confidence

1. Write a one- to two-page paper on the fall of communism in one eastern European country.

2. Do a report or paper on Ronald Reagan, George Bush, Deng Xiaoping, Mikhail Gorbachev or Manuel Noriega.

3. Pretend you are a reporter and do a newscast on the fall of the Berlin Wall.

4. Read old newpapers and magazines on the massacre in Tiananmen Square. Discuss your findings in class.

5. Make a time line of the Cold War. Discuss in class what the Cold War accomplished.

6. Discuss terrorism in class. Why do people do it? Does it work?

7. Read about the invasion of Panama or Grenada.

8. Do some research and a report on the changes in China since Mao Zedong died.

9. Explore the Internet by searching "Cold War Museum."

Section 3: After the Cold War

1. Build a model of the attack on Kuwait.

2. Have a Persian Gulf veteran speak to your class about the war.

3. Do a one- to two-page paper on Bill Clinton, Norman Schwarzkopf, Colin Powell or Boris Yeltsin.

4. Make a graph of the deficits between 1975 and this year. On it, put how much the current national debt is.

5. Follow a current national news story in the paper for two weeks. Then, do a report on it in classs. Write how you think it will be reported in the history books in the future.

6. Read magazine articles on the invasion of Somalia or the threat to invade Haiti. Report to the class on what you find out.

7. Do an oral report or paper on life in one of the remaining communist countries.

8. Discuss these questions:

    a. What does it mean to have free trade?

    b. Why didn't the U.S. want to get involved in Yugoslavia?

    c. What made the Persian Gulf War such a success?

    d. Did the end of communism solve all the problems in the world?

9. Read about life in Cuba today and report to the class.

10. Explore the Internet by searching "Operation Desert Storm."

Administer the LIFEPAC Test.

The test is to be administered in one session. Give no help except with directions.
Evaluate the tests and review areas where the students have done poorly.
Review the pages and activities that stress the concepts tested.
If necessary, administer the Alternate LIFEPAC Test.

ANSWER KEYS

SECTION 1

1.1	China; U.S.S.R.
1.2	Henry Kissinger
1.3	1971
1.4	Leonid Brezhnev
1.5	Détente
1.6	technology
1.7	Strategic Arms Limitation Treaty
1.8	containment
1.9	1979
1.10	television
1.11	communists
1.12	Watergate
1.13	Archibald Cox
1.14	Spiro Agnew
1.15	Gerald Ford
1.16	*Washington Post*
1.17	August 9, 1974
1.18	Committee to Re-elect the President
1.19	John Dean
1.20	Jimmy Carter
1.21	He pardoned Richard Nixon.
1.22	Electronic listening devices; bugs
1.23	He had no experience in the federal government that people distrusted so much.
1.24	The tape recordings he made in his own office.
1.25	inflation; energy crisis
1.26	embargoed
1.27	Camp David Accords
1.28	Afghanistan
1.29	Iran Hostage
1.30	Islam
1.31	Organization of Petroleum Exporting Countries
1.32	Federal Reserve Board
1.33	Ronald Reagan

SELF TEST 1

1.01	c
1.02	j
1.03	i
1.04	d
1.05	e
1.06	a
1.07	h
1.08	g
1.09	b
1.010	f
1.011	Watergate
1.012	Any order: U.S.S.R., China
1.013	Détente
1.014	Any order: inflation, energy crisis
1.015	Camp David
1.016	Strategic Arms Limitation Treaty
1.017	Iran Hostage Crisis
1.018	Afghanistan
1.019	false
1.020	false
1.021	true
1.022	true
1.023	true
1.024	false
1.025	true
1.026	false
1.027	false
1.028	false

SECTION 2

2.1	They kill, bomb, and kidnap to force people to give them what they want.
2.2	The end of the Iran Hostage Crisis
2.3	social programs
2.4	the military
2.5	A truck loaded with explosives was driven into their barracks in Lebanon, killing about 200 people.
2.6	Iran was at war with Iraq and needed its money being held in the U.S.
2.7	The Sandinistas were the communist government of Nicaragua. The Contras were fighting against them.
2.8	The president sold weapons to Iran and some of the money was illegally sent to the Contras.
2.9	The U.S. invaded to overthrow a communist government there. A free government was set up instead.
2.10	Tiananmen; army
2.11	Deng Xiaoping
2.12	Three
2.13	Mikhail Gorbachev
2.14	*perestroika; glasnost*
2.15	Afghanistan
2.16	cut back or reduced
2.17	summit
2.18	They were given back to the people, who ran them as they chose to make money.
2.19	He would not use the Soviet army to protect communism there.
2.20	To make the U.S.S.R. a richer and more powerful communist nation.
2.21	It was too expensive for the Soviet Union.
2.22	Savings and Loan
2.23	1989
2.24	Solidarity
2.25	Panama
2.26	Manuel Noriega
2.27	George H. W. Bush
2.28	Communism fell in much of eastern Europe and the Cold War ended.
2.29	Its people were leaving to go to West Germany through Hungary.

SELF TEST 2

2.01	The Cold War ended and communism fell in much of eastern Europe. Any two: The dictator of Romania was killed and a non-communist government set up. The Czechoslovakian government was turned over to non-communists. Poland signed an agreement with Solidarity which won all the free elections. Hungary renounced communism and opened its borders. East Germany opened its borders with West Germany, and the Berlin Wall came down.
2.02	The Committee to Re-elect the President paid men to break into the Democratic headquarters. The President told his people to cover up their part in it. The cover up was proven by the tapes Nixon made in his office. He resigned.
2.03	Businesses and farms were given back to people who ran them as they pleased to make money.
2.04	Ronald Reagan
2.05	war
2.06	Nicaragua
2.07	Grenada
2.08	the army
2.09	openness
2.010	Afghanistan
2.011	Savings and Loan
2.012	Panama
2.013	summit
2.014	i
2.015	b
2.016	h
2.017	c
2.018	l
2.019	g
2.020	e
2.021	k
2.022	d
2.023	f
2.024	j
2.025	a
2.026	true
2.027	false
2.028	true
2.029	true
2.030	false
2.031	true
2.032	true
2.033	true
2.034	false
2.035	true

2.036 true
2.037 true
2.038 false

SECTION 3

3.1   Saddam Hussein
3.2   Kuwait
3.3   George H. W. Bush
3.4   100
3.5   United Nations
3.6   Saudi Arabia
3.7   true
3.8   true
3.9   false
3.10 false
3.11 false
3.12 true
3.13 true
3.14 true
3.15 false
3.16 true
3.17 false
3.18 true
3.19 true
3.20 false
3.21 false
3.22 Yugoslavia
3.23 NAFTA
3.24 Croatia, Bosnia (either order); Kosovo
3.25 deficits
3.26 Cuba
3.27 Haiti
3.28 Bill Clinton
3.29 Cuba
3.30 Jimmy Carter
3.31 European Union
3.32 lied
3.33 four
3.34 Kyoto
3.35 Afghanistan
3.36 Mercy
3.37 Osama bin Laden
3.38 Indian
3.39 the Sudan
3.40 Bill Clinton
3.41 Darfur
3.42 Iraq

SELF TEST 3

3.01	h
3.02	i
3.03	g
3.04	a
3.05	b
3.06	f
3.07	e
3.08	d
3.09	c
3.010	Desert Storm or Persian Gulf War
3.011	deficits
3.012	NAFTA
3.013	Yugoslavia
3.014	Any one: Vietnam, China, North Korea, Cuba
3.015	Iran Hostage
3.016	Watergate
3.017	George W. Bush
3.018	Osama bin Laden
3.019	Indian Ocean
3.020	Japan
3.021	Sudan
3.022	To take over its oil wealth and add to Hussein's power
3.023	They tried and failed to take over the government and restore communist power.
3.024	The dictators could no longer get aid by picking sides in the Cold War.
3.025	To allow food to be delivered to the people in the country who were starving.
3.026	It divided into fifteen countries.
3.027	The Savings and Loans failed and the government which insured them had to pay for the money that was lost.
3.028	Communism ended in eastern Europe and the Cold War ended.
3.029	The Strategic Arms Limitation Treaty; it slowed the nuclear arms race down.
3.030	Farms and businesses were given to the people to run and make money for themselves.
3.031	false
3.032	true
3.033	false
3.034	false
3.035	true
3.036	false
3.037	false
3.038	true
3.039	true
3.040	true

LIFEPAC TEST

1.	false; change <u>Desert</u> to <u>Persian Gulf</u>
2.	false; change <u>Iran-Contra Affair</u> to <u>Iran Hostage Crisis</u>
3.	true
4.	false; change <u>Hungary</u> to <u>Cuba</u>, <u>Vietnam</u> or <u>North Korea</u>
5.	false; change <u>deficits</u> to <u>inflation</u>
6.	true
7.	false; change <u>SALT</u> to <u>Camp David Accords</u>
8.	true
9.	false; change <u>Poland</u> to <u>Afghanistan</u>
10.	false; change <u>Yugoslavia</u> to <u>China</u>
11.	China
12.	U.S.S.R. (Soviet Union)
13.	1989
14.	Haiti
15.	Yugoslavia
16.	Watergate
17.	OPEC
18.	Watergate
19.	Lebanon
20.	pardon
21.	Darfur
22.	Afghanistan
23.	Indian Ocean
24.	f
25.	e
26.	b
27.	b
28.	c
29.	a
30.	f
31.	g
32.	d
33.	a
34.	e
35.	e
36.	b
37.	i
38.	j
39.	c
40.	h
41.	g
42.	d
43.	f
44.	a

ALTERNATE LIFEPAC TEST

1.   k
2.   d
3.   r
4.   g
5.   a
6.   n
7.   o
8.   t
9.   h
10.   b
11.   q
12.   s
13.   f
14.   c
15.   e
16.   p
17.   i
18.   j
19.   l
20.   m
21.   Communism ended all over eastern Europe and the Cold War ended.
22.   Iran went to war with Iraq and needed the money held in America until the hostages were released.
23.   They were attacked and driven out by the Chinese army.
24.   War with Iran had left Iraq deeply in debt. Dictator Saddam Hussein owed money to the oil-rich nation of Kuwait. Iraq and Kuwait disagreed over the location of their border and who could pump oil from underground oil sources that were beneath both countries. Hussein also claimed that Kuwait was really a part of Iraq and used all these things as excuses to invade Kuwait in August of 1990 to take over their oil wealth.
25.   false
26.   true
27.   true
28.   false
29.   true
30.   true
31.   true
32.   false
33.   true
34.   true
35.   false
36.   false
37.   true

38.   i
39.   j
40.   h
41.   l
42.   c
43.   d
44.   a
45.   m
46.   b
47.   e

HISTORY & GEOGRAPHY 509

ALTERNATE LIFEPAC TEST

NAME _____

DATE _____

SCORE _____

Match these items (each answer, 2 points).

1. _____ Reagan ordered this island invaded to overthrow a communist government

2. _____ Reagan sold weapons to Iran and the money was used to fight the Sandinistas in Nicaragua

3. _____ Split apart into 15 countries in 1991

4. _____ Organization of nations that export oil

5. _____ War to free Kuwait from Iraq

6. _____ Basis of peace between Israel and Egypt

7. _____ Time in the 1970s when gas prices rose and shortages occurred

8. _____ Reform of openness in the Soviet Union

9. _____ Treaty to limit atomic weapons

10. _____ 52 diplomats held prisoner for 444 days

11. _____ Communist country that gave businesses and farms back to the people in the 1970s and '80s

12. _____ Trade agreement between U.S., Canada, and Mexico

13. _____ Operation that included intense bombing of Iraq

14. _____ Was a big problem in the 1970s, was brought under control by the Federal Reserve Board

15. _____ President's aides hired burglars to break into the Democratic headquarters, cover-up proven by recordings made by the president in his office

16. _____ Thaw in the Cold War in the 1970s, begun by Richard Nixon visits to China and the Soviet Union

17. _____ Nation invaded by the Soviet Union in 1979, they withdrew in 1988 and 1989

18. _____ Invaded by the U.S. to overthrow drug smuggling military leader

19. _____ Island threatened with invasion under Bill Clinton to restore the elected president

20. _____ Crisis under George H. W. Bush, government had to pay billions for closed banks

a. Persian Gulf
b. Iran Hostage Crisis
c. inflation
d. Iran-Contra Affair
e. Watergate
f. Desert Storm
g. OPEC
h. SALT
i. Afghanistan
j. Panama
k. Grenada
l. Haiti
m. Savings and Loan
n. Camp David Accords
o. energy crisis
p. Détente
q. China
r. U.S.S.R.
s. NAFTA
t. *glasnost*

Answer these questions (each answer, 4 points).

21.   Why was 1989 a miracle year? _____

_____

_____

_____

22.   Why did the Iran Hostage Crisis end? _____

_____

_____

23.   What happened to the students who protested in Tiananmen Square? _____

_____

_____

24.   Why did Iraq invade Kuwait? _____

_____

_____

_____

_____

Answer *true* or *false* (each answer, 2 points).

25.   _____   The U.S.S.R. invaded Somalia to help the communist government there in 1994.

26.   _____   Yugoslavia had divided into several countries, and its people have fought among themselves since the Cold War.

27.   _____   North Korea and Cuba were still communist after the Cold War.

28.   _____   Darfur is a relatively peaceful region in Africa.

29.   _____   Terrorists blew up a Marine barracks in Lebanon in 1983, killing over 200 American service men.

30.   _____   Al Qaeda was responsible for the terrorist attacks on the U.S.

31.   _____   The U.S.-led coalition invaded Kuwait along its border and to the north through Iraq in the Persian Gulf War.

32.   _____   The U.S. was the first nation to sign the Kyoto Protocol.

33. _____ The U.S. has not wanted to get deeply involved in the wars in the former Yugoslavia.

34. _____ The Iraqi army set Kuwait's oil wells on fire as they retreated.

35. _____ A tsunami is a large flood that happens after a piece of the Antarctic ice shelf drops into the sea.

36. _____ President Jimmy Carter forced the Soviet Union to withdraw from eastern Europe.

37. _____ On September 11, 2001, four planes were hijacked to be used as weapons.

Match these people (each answer, 2 points).

38. _____ President who opposed communism and wanted to cut government control

39. _____ President during the September 11, 2001, terrorist attacks

40. _____ Last president of the Soviet Union, began the reforms that ended it

41. _____ Second president impeached

42. _____ Leader of the Al Qaeda terrorist organization

43. _____ President during the Iran Hostage Crisis, his lack of experience in Washington got him elected

44. _____ President who resigned from office

45. _____ Leader of Iraq during the Persian Gulf War

46. _____ Appointed president, became unpopular for pardoning the president before him

47. _____ Secretary of State under Nixon

a. Richard Nixon

b. Gerald Ford

c. Osama bin Laden

d. Jimmy Carter

e. Henry Kissinger

f. Boris Yeltsin

g. Barack Obama

h. Mikhail Gorbachev

i. Ronald Reagan

j. George W. Bush

k. George H. W. Bush

l. Bill Clinton

m. Saddam Hussein

HISTORY & GEOGRAPHY 510

Unit 10: The United States of America

TEACHER NOTES

MATERIALS NEEDED FOR LIFEPAC	
Required	Suggested
(None)	• world map

ADDITIONAL LEARNING ACTIVITIES

1. Make flash cards for important people, events or wars.

2. Make a time line of U.S. history.

3. Quiz each other: Give three to five events in America's history and have the student put them in chronological order.

4. Memorize the names of the presidents for extra credit.

5. Discuss these questions:

    a. What was the most important event in U.S. history?

    b. Who was the most important person in U.S. history?

    c. How is America different today from what it was like in 1776? in 1890?

    d. How did each American war change the country?

    e. If you had to live back in American history before 1920, when would you live and why?

6. Read the U.S. Constitutional Amendments and discuss why each was added.

7. Read a book about your favorite topic in U.S. history.

8. Draw a picture of your favorite event in U.S. history.

Administer the LIFEPAC Test.

The test is to be administered in one session. Give no help except with directions.
Evaluate the tests and review areas where the students have done poorly.
Review the pages and activities that stress the concepts tested.
If necessary, administer the Alternate LIFEPAC Test.

ANSWER KEYS

SECTION 1

1.1	Magellan
1.2	Jacques Cartier
1.3	Henry Hudson
1.4	Christopher Columbus
1.5	Leif Ericson
1.6	John Cabot
1.7	Samuel de Champlain
1.8	Ponce de Leon
1.9	Henry the Navigator
1.10	Hernando de Soto
1.11	Francis Drake
1.12	Francisco Coronado
1.13	Louis Jolliet and Jacques Marquette
1.14	Sieur de la Salle
1.15	spices
1.16	fur
1.17	Northwest Passage
1.18	Great; Mississippi
1.19	Connecticut
1.20	South Carolina
1.21	Massachusetts
1.22	Georgia
1.23	Virginia
1.24	North Carolina
1.25	Rhode Island
1.26	Any order: Delaware, Pennsylvania
1.27	Maryland
1.28	New Jersey
1.29	New York
1.30	French and Indian
1.31	Intolerable Acts
1.32	Proclamation of 1763
1.33	Boston Tea Party
1.34	Second Continental Congress
1.35	Stamp Act Congress

1.36	Townshend Acts
1.37	Declaratory Act
1.38	Lexington
1.39	First Continental Congress
1.40	Stamp Act
1.41	Bunker Hill
1.42	Declaration of Independence
1.43	Any order: Saratoga, Yorktown
1.44	Ticonderoga
1.45	Valley Forge; von Stuben
1.46	Nathanael Greene
1.47	Benedict Arnold
1.48	George Washington
1.49	Trenton; Hessians
1.50	Saratoga
1.51	Mississippi River
1.52	George Rogers Clark
1.53	farmers
1.54	cotton gin; interchangeable parts
1.55	Samuel Slater
1.56	Any order: fishing, whaling, shipbuilding
1.57	rum; slaves; Middle; molasses
1.58	Any order: slaves, land
1.59	There was no president or federal courts. Congress could not tax or control trade.
1.60	States with more people would have more votes in the House, but all states would have the same vote in the Senate.
1.61	Gave every territory the right to become a state when it had 60,000 people
1.62	Any order: legislative, judicial, executive
1.63	a. Federalists b. Anti-Federalists
1.64	First ten Amendments to the Constitution
1.65	James Madison
1.66	George Washington
1.67	George Washington
1.68	The French refused to negotiate with the U.S. without a bribe.
1.69	Laws to make it harder to become a citizen and illegal to criticize the government
1.70	Democratic-Republicans, Thomas Jefferson; Federalists, Alexander Hamilton
1.71	a. John Adams b. Thomas Jefferson
1.72	The South got it in exchange for allowing the federal government to take over state war debts.
1.73	War Hawks

1.74 Louisiana Purchase
1.75 Battle of Lake Erie
1.76 embargo
1.77 Ghent
1.78 Oliver Perry
1.79 Lewis and Clark Expedition
1.80 Tecumseh
1.81 McHenry
1.82 "Star Spangled Banner"
1.83 impressment
1.84 Tippecanoe
1.85 Washington, D.C.
1.86 impressment, taking of U.S. cargoes, British forts in U.S. land and the British were giving guns to the Indians
1.87 Robert Fulton; *Clermont*; 1807
1.88 Battle of New Orleans; Andrew Jackson
1.89 Democrats and Whigs
1.90 nationalism, manufacturing
1.91 European nations could not take more American colonies, that would threaten the U.S.
1.92 National or Cumberland Road
1.93 Erie Canal; connected Lake Erie with the Mohawk and Hudson Rivers
1.94 Adams-Onis Treaty; Andrew Jackson
1.95 No slavery in the Louisiana Purchase north of 36° 30', Maine admitted as a free state, Missouri as a slave one
1.96 a. high tariffs, high federal land prices, no slavery in the territories, no federal money for roads or canals
   b. low tariffs, slavery in the territories, no federal money for roads/canals
   c. low federal land prices, federal money for roads/canals

SELF TEST 1

1.01 n
1.02 j
1.03 l
1.04 b
1.05 o
1.06 c
1.07 a
1.08 e
1.09 i
1.010 d
1.011 m
1.012 f
1.013 k
1.014 h
1.015 g
1.016 Mississippi
1.017 New York
1.018 Virginia
1.019 French and Indian
1.020 Lexington
1.021 Yorktown
1.022 Boston Tea Party
1.023 War of 1812
1.024 Louisiana Purchase
1.025 Bill of Rights
1.026 h
1.027 d
1.028 i
1.029 g
1.030 e
1.031 o
1.032 c
1.033 l
1.034 j
1.035 f
1.036 b
1.037 m
1.038 a
1.039 n
1.040 k
1.041 true
1.042 false
1.043 false
1.044 true
1.045 false
1.046 false
1.047 false
1.048 true
1.049 false
1.050 false

SECTION 2

2.1	Andrew Jackson	2.42	North (Union); South (Confederacy)
2.2	William Henry Harrison	2.43	Fort Sumter; Gettysburg; Appomattox Courthouse
2.3	Andrew Jackson		
2.4	Martin Van Buren	2.44	Abraham Lincoln; Jefferson Davis
2.5	John Tyler	2.45	Emancipation Proclamation; 13th
2.6	James Polk	2.46	Andrew Johnson; Ten Percent
2.7	Andrew Jackson	2.47	Radical Republicans
2.8	William Henry Harrison	2.48	14th; 15th
2.9	James Polk	2.49	Carpetbaggers; Scalawags
2.10	Andrew Jackson	2.50	violence; Democratic
2.11	Andrew Jackson	2.51	1877; Rutherford B. Hayes
2.12	John Tyler	2.52	Gilded
2.13	James Polk	2.53	Homestead
2.14	James Polk	2.54	1869
2.15	James Buchanan	2.55	steel; oil
2.16	Abraham Lincoln	2.56	Alexander Bell; Thomas Edison
2.17	Zachary Taylor	2.57	Pendleton; railroads
2.18	c	2.58	tariffs; railroads
2.19	i	2.59	trust
2.20	k	2.60	corruption
2.21	l	2.61	Archduke Ferdinand, the Austrian heir, was assassinated in Sarajevo
2.22	g		
2.23	j	2.62	the U.S. battleship *Maine* blew up in Havana harbor
2.24	f		
2.25	g	2.63	Progressive Era
2.26	h	2.64	Germany began unrestricted submarine warfare on ships trading with the Allies
2.27	h		
2.28	b	2.65	Any order: Theodore Roosevelt, William Taft, Woodrow Wilson
2.29	e		
2.30	g	2.66	Roaring Twenties
2.31	c	2.67	Prohibition
2.32	d	2.68	League of Nations
2.33	m	2.69	Spanish-American War
2.34	a	2.70	Stock Market Crash of 1929
2.35	c	2.71	Fourteen Points
2.36	e	2.72	credit
2.37	j	2.73	John Pershing
2.38	k	2.74	Germany
2.39	a		
2.40	b		
2.41	Ulysses S. Grant; Robert E. Lee		

SELF TEST 2

2.01	e
2.02	m
2.03	o
2.04	j
2.05	f
2.06	g
2.07	d
2.08	n
2.09	b
2.010	k
2.011	h
2.012	c
2.013	l
2.014	a
2.015	i
2.016	Spanish-American War
2.017	World War I
2.018	War for Texas Independence
2.019	Mexican War
2.020	Civil War
2.021	h
2.022	o
2.023	g
2.024	m
2.025	a
2.026	k
2.027	n
2.028	e
2.029	j
2.030	d
2.031	b
2.032	f
2.033	l
2.034	i
2.035	c
2.036	The belief that America's obvious future was to spread across the continent
2.037	End slavery in the U.S.
2.038	It showed slaves as suffering people and turned the North against slavery.
2.039	It gave government jobs to people who did the best on a special test.
2.040	He vetoed its charter and moved out federal money to pet banks so the National Bank closed.
2.041	A
2.042	D
2.043	F
2.044	C
2.045	B

SECTION 3

3.1	New Deal
3.2	Germany invaded Poland
3.3	1 out of 4
3.4	World War II
3.5	Axis Powers
3.6	Jews
3.7	Atlantic Charter
3.8	Benito Mussolini
3.9	Adolf Hitler
3.10	Winston Churchill
3.11	Vichy France
3.12	Lend-Lease
3.13	Japanese attack on Pearl Harbor
3.14	Battle of the Atlantic
3.15	Invading the U.S.S.R. without preparing for winter
3.16	Stalingrad
3.17	Any order: North Africa, Italy and Normandy (France)
3.18	D-Day
3.19	Holocaust
3.20	Douglas MacArthur
3.21	Coral Sea
3.22	Midway
3.23	Island Hopping
3.24	Manhattan Project
3.25	Franklin D. Roosevelt
3.26	United Nations
3.27	Harry Truman
3.28	Any order: Hiroshima, Nagasaki
3.29	Communism
3.30	Iron Curtain
3.31	Marshall Plan
3.32	Berlin Airlift
3.33	Douglas MacArthur
3.34	Chiang Kai-shek; Mao Zedong
3.35	Berlin Wall
3.36	Joseph McCarthy
3.37	Sputnik; U.S.S.R.
3.38	Cuban Missile
3.39	Vietnam
3.40	Gulf of Tonkin
3.41	Richard Nixon
3.42	Civil Rights Movement
3.43	Vietnam War
3.44	rebelled
3.45	John Kennedy
3.46	Lyndon Johnson
3.47	Dwight Eisenhower
3.48	Martin Luther King, Jr.; Montgomery Bus Boycott

3.49	false
3.50	true
3.51	false
3.52	true
3.53	true
3.54	false
3.55	true
3.56	true
3.57	true
3.58	true
3.59	false
3.60	false
3.61	true
3.62	false
3.63	false
3.64	false
3.65	false
3.66	true
3.67	false
3.68	false
3.69	false
3.70	false
3.71	true
3.72	true
3.73	false
3.74	true
3.75	false

SELF TEST 3

3.01	g
3.02	l
3.03	n
3.04	i
3.05	f
3.06	b
3.07	o
3.08	a
3.09	h
3.010	e
3.011	k
3.012	d
3.013	m
3.014	c
3.015	j
3.016	Great Depression
3.017	Holocaust
3.018	Pearl Harbor
3.019	Vietnam War
3.020	Iron Curtain
3.021	Cold War
3.022	Iran Hostage Crisis
3.023	Kuwait
3.024	Afghanistan
3.025	Normandy (France)
3.026	Afghanistan
3.027	Saddam Hussein
3.028	Barack Obama
3.029	true
3.030	false
3.031	true
3.032	true
3.033	true
3.034	false
3.035	true
3.036	true
3.037	true
3.038	true
3.039	i
3.040	h
3.041	a
3.042	f
3.043	j
3.044	b
3.045	e
3.046	d
3.047	c
3.048	g

LIFEPAC TEST

1. Spanish-American War
2. War of 1812
3. World War II
4. Revolutionary War
5. World War I
6. Great Depression
7. Vietnam War
8. Mexican War
9. Civil War
10. French and Indian War
11. j
12. e
13. a
14. c
15. i
16. h
17. d
18. b
19. f
20. g
21. g
22. n
23. e
24. t
25. r
26. m
27. q
28. a
29. p
30. o
31. i
32. s
33. h
34. c
35. d
36. b
37. l
38. f
39. j
40. k
41. false
42. false
43. true
44. true
45. false
46. false
47. false
48. true
49. false
50. false
51. false
52. true
53. false

ALTERNATE LIFEPAC TEST

1. j
2. k
3. p
4. a
5. r
6. f
7. c
8. u
9. x
10. t
11. v
12. m
13. h
14. n
15. y
16. l
17. b
18. i
19. o
20. q
21. w
22. g
23. e
24. d
25. s
26. n
27. d
28. a
29. h
30. o
31. b
32. c
33. m
34. l
35. i
36. g
37. k
38. j
39. f
40. e
41. true
42. true
43. false
44. false
45. false
46. true
47. false
48. false
49. false
50. true
51. false
52. true
53. false

HISTORY & GEOGRAPHY 510

ALTERNATE LIFEPAC TEST

NAME _____

DATE _____

SCORE _____

$$\frac{85}{106}$$

Match these items (each answer, 2 points).

1. _____ Time of fun and spending after World War I
2. _____ Land bought from France west of the Mississippi
3. _____ Movement to end slavery
4. _____ War to free Kuwait from Iraq
5. _____ Turning point of the Civil War
6. _____ Colonist's response to tax on tea
7. _____ War, U.S. recognized as a world power, 1898
8. _____ War to end slavery in the U.S.
9. _____ First battle of the Revolutionary War
10. _____ Scandal that forced a president to resign
11. _____ Federalists wanted it, Anti-Federalists did not
12. _____ First British colony in America
13. _____ Nation freed by Theodore Roosevelt to build a canal, invaded by George H. W. Bush to arrest a drug smuggler
14. _____ Gold rush gave it enough people for statehood, the Compromise of 1850 got it into the Union
15. _____ War with Britain over impressment
16. _____ State that was an independent republic for nine years after defeating Santa Anna at San Jacinto
17. _____ Long, controversial war, protested at home, Richard Nixon got the U.S. out of it
18. _____ Murder of millions, especially Jews, by the Nazis
19. _____ Supreme Court made slavery legal in all of America
20. _____ Turning point of the Pacific War, World War II
21. _____ Began with the Stock Market Crash of 1929, the New Deal helped people with it
22. _____ World War II ally, Cold War enemy
23. _____ James Polk started this war to get California, got the whole Mexican Cession
24. _____ Crisis, 52 diplomats held for 444 days
25. _____ Began when Archduke Ferdinand was assassinated

a. Persian Gulf
b. Vietnam
c. Spanish-American
d. Iran Hostage
e. Mexican War
f. Boston Tea Party
g. Soviet Union
h. Panama
i. Holocaust
j. Roaring Twenties
k. Louisiana Purchase
l. Texas
m. Virginia
n. California
o. Dred Scott
p. Abolition
q. Midway
r. Gettysburg
s. World War I
t. Watergate
u. Civil War
v. Constitution
w. Great Depression
x. Lexington
y. War of 1812

Match these people (each answer, 2 points).

26. _____ Inventor of the telegraph

27. _____ Only appointed president

28. _____ Communist Chinese leader

29. _____ Revolutionary hero and traitor

30. _____ Inventor of the light bulb and the phonograph

31. _____ President, spoils system, Nullification Crisis, hero of the Battle of New Orleans

32. _____ First president to visit the U.S.S.R. and China

33. _____ Progressive president, Fourteen Points

34. _____ Confederate general

35. _____ Last Soviet president, allowed communism to end in eastern Europe

36. _____ Founded Rhode Island

37. _____ Gave the Dutch a claim in New Netherlands which became New York

38. _____ Anti-communist president, invaded Grenada

39. _____ Civil War commander of the Union army

40. _____ U.S. general, World War II and Korean War

a. Mao Zedong

b. Andrew Jackson

c. Richard Nixon

d. Gerald Ford

e. Douglas MacArthur

f. Ulysses S. Grant

g. Roger Williams

h. Benedict Arnold

i. Mikhail Gorbachev

j. Ronald Reagan

k. Henry Hudson

l. Robert E. Lee

m. Woodrow Wilson

n. Samuel Morse

o. Thomas Edison

Write *true* or *false* in the blank (each answer, 2 points).

41. _____ Rhode Island, New Hampshire, and Georgia were among the original thirteen colonies.

42. _____ Thomas Hooker, William Penn, and James Oglethorpe founded British colonies in America.

43. _____ The Stamp Act and Declaratory Act made the colonists feel good about having Britain rule them.

44. _____ The Cuban Missile Crisis and the Bay of Pigs were part of the Spanish-American War.

45. _____ Richard Nixon was the only U.S. president impeached.

46. _____ Columbus, Magellan, and Ponce de Leon all worked for Spain when they explored the New World.

47. _____ The League of Nations was created to protect world peace after the Vietnam War.

48. _____ The Holocaust by the Nazis was aimed mainly at Africans.

49. _____ The New Deal ended the Great Depression.

50. _____ The Cold War ended when communism fell in Europe in 1989.

51. _____ The U.S. had never experienced a terrorist attack before September 11, 2001.

52. _____ Osama bin Laden headed the Al Qaeda terrorist group.

53. _____ The U.S. decided against invading Iraq and removing Saddam Hussein from power.